HF6161.C35F7 197

DUE

FRITSCHLE
SMOKING & P
MAKING & TH

DATE DUE			
? 1 8 '8U	MAY 1 3 '98		
10/8/81	DEC 1 3 '00		
OCT 1 3 1981	EC 1 3 00		
NOV 2 6 '86			
5/4/27			
APR 22 '92			
DEC 2 '9			
MAY 09 '94			
MR 2 5 96			
OCT 1 4 '97	'98		
OCT 2 0 '97			

SECOND EDITION

SMOKING AND POLITICS

Policymaking and the Federal Bureaucracy

A. LEE FRITSCHLER
The American University

Prentice-Hall, Inc., *Englewood Cliffs, New Jersey*

Library of Congress Cataloging in Publication Data

FRITSCHLER, A. LEE
    Smoking and politics.

    Bibliography: p.
      1. Cigarettes—Labeling—United States. 2. Adver-
tising—Cigarettes. 3. United States. Federal Trade
Commission. I. Title.
HF6161.C35F7 1975   659.1'9'67973   74–12381
ISBN 0–13–815019–2

FOR ALICEANN

10 9 8 7 6 5 4 3 2 1

Prentice-Hall International, Inc., *London*
Prentice-Hall of Australia, Pty. Ltd., *Sydney*
Prentice-Hall of Canada, Ltd., *Toronto*
Prentice-Hall of India Private Limited, *New Delhi*
Prentice-Hall of Japan, Inc., *Tokyo*

CONTENTS

PREFACE   *v*

1   CIGARETTES AND THE POLICY PROCESS   *1*
Tobacco Power   Nicotania: The Beginnings of the Controversy
A Challenge to the Subsystem   Administrative Policymaking
Bureaucrats and Congressmen

2   SMOKING AND ADMINISTRATIVE POLITICS   *17*
Research Uncovers a Health Hazard   Industry's Response
Birth of a Lobby   Tobacco in the Economy
Congress Rebuffs Health Proponents   Smokers Sue Manufacturers
Bureaucratic Conflict

3   THE ADVISORY COMMITTEE AND THE NEW POLICY
DIRECTIONS   *37*
Advisory Committees in the Bureaucracy
The Surgeon General's Committee at Work
The Advisory Committee's Report   Controlling Advisory Committees

4   DEVELOPMENT OF ADMINISTRATIVE
POLICYMAKING POWERS   *53*
Regulatory Authority Delegated to Federal Trade Commission
The Supreme Court on Delegation   Change in Emphasis at the FTC

5 PROCEDURES USED IN ADMINISTRATIVE POLICYMAKING *70*

Adjudication and Rulemaking at the FTC
The Federal Trade Commission's Experience with Cigarette Regulation
The Federal Trade Commission Adopts Rulemaking Procedures
The Administrative Procedure Act   The Federal Register

6 THE RULEMAKING HEARINGS *88*

Cigarette Hearings at the Federal Trade Commission   Witnesses
Position of the Industry   The Commissioners Respond
The Federal Trade Commission's Defense of its Action
Administrative Law Judges (Hearing Examiners)
Promulgation of Rules   Tobacco Interests Object to the Rule
Judicial Review of Administrative Actions

7 CONGRESSIONAL POWER AND AGENCY POLICYMAKING *115*

Congressional Oversight
The Federal Trade Commission's Oversight Struggle
No Victory for Health   Strategy for Success   The Health Lobby
The Congressional Hearings   The Cigarette Men Testify
The Federal Trade Commission Rescinds its Rule

8 CONGRESS AND THE BUREAUCRACY: A BALANCE OF POWER? *140*

Bureaucracy Continues the Controversy
The Bureaucracy and Congress in Policymaking

appendix I CHRONOLOGY OF IMPORTANT EVENTS IN THE CIGARETTE LABELING CONTROVERSY *157*

appendix II FEDERAL TRADE COMMISSION'S TRADE REGULATION RULE ON CIGARETTE LABELING AND ADVERTISING (29 FR 8325) *169*

SUGGESTIONS FOR FURTHER READINGS *172*

INDEX *176*

PREFACE

PREFACE TO THE SECOND EDITION

The processes of agency policymaking illustrated by the cigarette labeling controversy are being used more and more frequently by well-organized, highly skilled groups representing consumer interests. Citizen advocates at all levels of government have discovered that change can be brought about by manipulation of the rules and regulations that govern agencies and by participating in the processes agencies follow to write rules. The use of agency powers is the cornerstone of the successes of the groups founded and inspired by Ralph Nader and his followers. They have started a movement. The movement puts the study of administrative law and administrative

politics high on the list of skills needed by a new breed of students
who wish to be activists. Public participation in agency policy processes was minimal until recently. Now, bureaucracy-centered politics
is more fruitful both as a field of study and as a means of influencing
public policy than it was when the first edition of *Smoking and
Politics* appeared in 1969.

The second edition brings the controversy over the issue of
smoking and health up to date by covering the fascinating developments of the last five years. The book now benefits from new materials on policymaking processes and consumer politics. By including
recent events and new studies in political science, the second edition
provides the basis for further generalizations on agency policymaking. Some of these generalizations are made explicitly, but many are
left for the student to discover.

The revisions in this edition are extensive, although I have been
careful not to disturb the basic structure of the book and its analysis
of agency policymaking powers.

Once again I am grateful to many people for assisting me. My
colleague at American University, Carl Akins, read and re-read
every word of the manuscript and proposed excellent suggestions for
its improvement. Jerome J. Hanus from American gave me several
fine suggestions based on his use of the first edition in the classroom
and his own research in the field of public policy analysis. Another
colleague, Robert E. Cleary, not only used the book often but also
invited the author to his classroom to discuss it with his students on
several occasions. The results of those sessions are reflected in the
second edition.

I interviewed several people who have been participants in the
cigarette controversy over the years and active in other areas of bureaucratic policymaking. The time they gave me and the interest they
maintained in this work are very sincerely appreciated. Three individuals were especially helpful. Emil Corwin, information officer,
National Clearinghouse for Smoking and Health, U.S. Department
of Health, Education and Welfare, supplied me with much data and
background on the cigarette controversy; William Kloepfer, Jr.,
senior vice president, The Tobacco Institute, Inc., gave me a de-

tailed, fair-minded criticism of the manuscript; and Irving Schiller, administrative law judge, U.S. Securities and Exchange Commission, assisted me in analyzing the complicated judicial procedures used in administrative agencies.

My wife, Aliceann, performed the burdensome tasks of editorial criticism and consultant on policymaking in government agencies based on her experiences as a member of the federal affairs staff of the National Association of Counties in Washington. This she managed while humoring her husband and our two boys, Craig and Eric.

PREFACE TO THE FIRST EDITION

The bureaucracy is the focal point of the policymaking process in modern governments. Society relies upon bureaucracies to make policy decisions that in less complicated times were made by elected executives, legislators, and judges. These elected officials presently find themselves responding more and more frequently to the initiatives of bureaucrats and to decisions made by administrative agencies.

Although bureaucratic activities are the heart of the policymaking processes of modern governments, they are far from being of central importance in most government courses and curricula. This book attempts to correct that deficiency by providing students of government with some understanding of why bureaucracies have become important and how they operate in the policymaking process.

Too often the policymaking activities of bureaucracies are overlooked because the processes and procedures used by agencies are complex, complicated, usually quite dull, and conducted away from the glare of publicity. The primary reason for the ascendancy of agencies to power, that is, the technical complexity of modern society and the resulting intricacies of administrative procedures, is, ironically, the factor keeping students from devoting time and attention to these important governmental functions. The implications of accelerated depreciation accounting techniques for the electric power industry, for example, are tremendously important to industry and the public, but both the public and students of government should be forgiven if they find it impossible to give this complicated issue much concentrated attention.[1]

Centering upon the policymaking process, the present study explores a public controversy that affected millions of Americans but which few understood except for the personal dilemma it presented. While the use of cigarettes had often been damned by clerics and scorned by health experts, the citizen suddenly found his government requiring that a health warning appear in advertisements for and on packages of cigarettes. The controversy generated over the proposed requirement for a health warning label was different from most administrative controversies and offers an exceptionally good opportunity to study the processes of agency policymaking because it was basically uncomplicated. The issue, simply stated, was: should the government require cigarette manufacturers to inform consumers of the results of studies of the medical-scientific community that indict cigarette smoking as a possible cause of lung cancer and other diseases? The reader's attention is directed to internal agency procedures and the external relations of one agency to Congress, the president, the courts, interest groups, the general public, and other agencies. The interactions among these institutions and political forces are observable at nearly every stage of the labeling controversy.

The cigarette labeling issue broke forcefully into public view on January 11, 1964, when the Surgeon General released the report of the Advisory Committee on Smoking and Health. One week later the Federal Trade Commission (FTC) prepared a regulation requiring a health warning to appear in all cigarette advertising and on cigarette packages. The processes and procedures used to write this rule were not exactly the same as those used by all agencies in policymaking because these procedures differ slightly from agency to agency. Furthermore, most bureaucratic policymaking does not draw as much attention from the public, Congress, and interest groups as the labeling controversy did. The extra attention that this issue received serves a useful purpose for students, however, by pro-

[1] A book with the sensational title of *Overcharge* did bring this issue to public attention but without emphasizing the policymaking process. Lee Metcalf and Vic Reinemer, *Overcharge* (New York: McKay Books, 1967).

viding the opportunity to examine more ramifications of the policy process than might otherwise be possible.

Utilizing a policy issue involving a maximum number of public officials and institutions, the study illustrates the "whirlpool" or sub-system effect in public policy formation, a phenomenon explored by Ernest S. Griffith and others in their studies of Congress.[2] In this book the focus is on the bureaucracy. The rulemaking and adjudicatory procedures of the Federal Trade Commission are generally the same as those of other independent regulatory commissions or the cabinet-level executive departments. This substantial degree of similarity in procedures allows the student to gain insight into the process of bureaucratic policymaking regardless of which bureaucratic institution one selects for study. Also, the significance of bureaucratic power vis-à-vis other political institutions, democratic theory, and the policymaking process does not change as one moves from one administrative body to another. Although specifically concerned with one policy question and concentrating primarily on one regulatory commission, the study illustrates generally the procedures and politics of bureaucratic policy formulation in contemporary American government.

Much of the information in this book was obtained from interviews with participants in the cigarette labeling controversy in the bureaucracy, Congress, and interest groups. Their contributions appear throughout the text, but there are too many of these very cooperative people to thank individually. I hope they will accept this blanket expression of gratitude for their help.

The late Daniel M. Berman suggested I write a book on this subject. His friendship and encouragement have been of lasting importance to me.

My students provided me with opportunities to test some approaches to the study of policymaking and to experiment with language intended to simplify complex ideas. Students in The American University's Washington Semester and in the Washington programs

[2] See Ernest S. Griffith, *Congress: Its Contemporary Role,* Third Edition (New York: New York University Press, 1961), pp. 50–51; and, also by Griffith, *The Impasse of Democracy* (New York: Harrison-Hilton Books, 1939), p. 182.

of Earlham College and Monmouth College must have wondered why we spent so much time talking with political figures about smoking and politics. Now that they know why, I want them to know that their questions and seminar discussions contributed significantly to this book.

Two talented students deserve special mention. Harold C. Relyea, a graduate student in political science at American, worked with me at every stage of the preparation of this book. His perceptive comments and skillful research assistance were invaluable. John D. Trezise, a former A.U. undergraduate, prepared an excellent analysis of the cigarette bill that was especially helpful in preparing Chapter 7.

Four of my colleagues at American, Robert E. Cleary, Jerome J. Hanus, Douglas Harman, and Louis S. Loeb (now at Luther College in Iowa), read the manuscript and contributed significantly to its betterment. James E. Underwood of Union College in Schenectady, New York, and William W. Boyer of the University of Delaware also read the manuscript and offered many thoughtful suggestions that they will now find in the text. Joel Yohalem, an attorney, helped me to improve the book's style and content. Nearly every page is better thanks to his tireless review and sharp pencil. Joan Hamm of Evanston, Illinois, enhanced the book by breathing some life into the lumpy style of an inexperienced writer. Dean Emeritus Earl H. DeLong of the School of Government and Public Administration of The American University has my gratitude for making A.U. a better place to teach and write.

To my wife, Aliceann, I owe a special note of thanks for her editorial assistance and understanding. There were times when she must have thought it would be better to put up with a husband returned to smoking than an irritable writer returning to draft after draft of a slowly improving manuscript.

Although I gratefully acknowledge the help of all these people, I, of course, must accept responsibility for any errors of fact or interpretation that might appear in the text.

A. L. F.

Washington, D.C.

Tobacco is an evil weed.
The Devil himself sowed the seed.
It stains your teeth,
And scents your clothes
And makes a chimney of your nose!

ANONYMOUS CHILDREN'S RHYME,
19TH CENTURY

No pleasure can exceed
  the smoking of the weed.

PHRASE FROM 19TH CENTURY,
ADVERTISEMENT

This Indian Weed, now withered quite,
  Though green at noon, cut down at night,
    Shows thy decay—
    All flesh is hay:
Thus think, and smoke tobacco.

FROM "TOBACCO"
BY GEORGE WITHER (1588–1667)

1

CIGARETTES AND THE POLICY PROCESS

As the evening variety show ended and the late news was about to begin, a panorama of traffic signals, danger signs, and cautionary flashing lights danced across the television screen. A chest X ray appeared, a man coughed, and a voice announced, "We receive many warnings in our lives." The camera then closed in on a cigarette package so that the viewer could read, "Caution: Cigarette Smoking May Be Hazardous to Your Health."

Today there are no cigarette ads on television, though a few antismoking commercials continue to appear. The warning has been made more emphatic: "Warning: The Surgeon General Has Determined That Cigarette Smoking Is Dangerous to Your Health." It no longer appears only in small print on the side panel of cigarette packages. In 1972, it also began appearing in all advertising, billboards, newspapers, and magazines in the United States.

Since January, 1966, a health warning has been printed on all cigarette packages sold in this country, and the public has been deluged with various kinds of publicity about the ill effects of cigarette smoking. Even so, the American smoker, to whom all these messages have been addressed, has reacted slowly and a bit grudgingly. One year after the warning had appeared there was no evidence that cigarette sales had been adversely affected. In fact, sales increased by 716 billion cigarettes during that year. Two years later cigarette sales dropped slightly. Then a rising trend began and sales reached new high records each year beginning in 1971. Per capita consumption of cigarettes apparently fell slightly between 1966 and 1970 and has risen each year since then. The figure is about 4,000 cigarettes per year for the entire U.S. population over the age of 18 years. In the five-year period between 1965 and 1970, there was an estimated decrease of 1.9 million cigarette smokers in the United States. Many quit—though perhaps only temporarily—and some apparently decided never to start.[1] Whether or not there is any relationship between the estimated drop in smoking and the appearance of the health warnings is a matter of speculation.

There has been a much clearer relationship between the requirement of health warnings and major changes in tobacco politics. The quiet, gentlemanly folkways of tobacco politics grew turbulent when it appeared in 1964 that the government might be successful in its efforts to warn smokers about possible health hazards. The traditional procedures for resolving conflicts between tobacco producers and the government quickly changed. Health warn-

---

[1] Data on the sales and consumption of cigarettes are from the U.S. Internal Revenue Service according to the taxes levied as cigarettes leave the manufacturers' warehouses for the consumer market. Per capita figures combine Revenue Service data with Census Bureau estimates of population growth. Since part of the period under discussion is between the national census periods, the population figures are necessarily estimates. The National Center for Health Statistics, U.S. Public Health Service, took national surveys in 1964–65 and 1970. The estimated 1.9 million drop in the numbers of smokers in the United States is taken from the results of those surveys.

ings in advertising and changes in consumption are the widely visible results of a political process involving administrative agencies, Congress, the courts, organized health and tobacco interests, and the public. These institutions and actors are involved in a continuing controversy involving both politics and science. The processes used to separate fact from fiction and to determine which policy should be adopted by government are common to policymaking in the United States; the cigarette labeling controversy is a piece of modern political Americana.

The processes from which emerged the temporary and changing policies in the smoking and health controversy are characteristic of consumer or public interest politics as it developed and expanded in the 1960s. Public interest politics uses the policymaking powers of legislatures, bureaucracies, and the courts in patterns of conflict inducing strategies. These strategies confirm the observation that the institutions of government operate, alone and in concert, in ways which ill fit traditional separation-of-powers notions of how the policy process works.

The politics of cigarette labeling demonstrates how institutions with separate responsibilities in the framework of the Constitution cooperate, conflict, and form temporary alliances to achieve policy goals. Further, the controvery illustrates the central role of the bureaucracy as policy initiator and policymaker in modern society. While policymaking powers are shared among the three traditional constitutional divisions of government—the legislative, the executive, and the judiciary—one of these institutions is usually more powerful in the policymaking process than the other, depending on the nature of the issue. Frequently, when the issue involves matters of technical complexity and powerful special interest opposition, the bureaucracy plays the leading role but there is no fixed distribution of power. And even though one institution might play a leading role, it is clear that the policy process cannot function when one of the institutions encounters concentrated opposition from another. The Federal Trade Commission (FTC) discovered the truth of this statement when it encountered a Congress hostile to its proposals for cigarette health warnings.

TOBACCO SUBSYSTEM

What has come to be the normal relationship between the institutions of national government was typified by traditional, or pre-1964, tobacco politics. Policy was made in a spirit of friendly and quiet cooperation between small segments of Congress, the bureaucracy, and the interest group community. The coalition of these fragments is referred to in social science literature as a subsystem. The term *subsystem* describes a structure dependent upon a larger political entity but one that functions with a high degree of autonomy. A committee of Congress could be called a subsystem of the larger legislative system just as an agency might be referred to as a subsystem of the bureaucracy. The tobacco subsystem is different from these in that it is a more encompassing policy subsystem. It cuts across institutional lines and includes within it all groups and individuals who are making and influencing government decisions concerning cigarettes and tobacco.[2]

The tobacco subsystem included the paid representatives of tobacco growers, marketing organizations, and cigarette manufacturers; congressmen representing tobacco constituencies; the leading members of four subcommittees in Congress—two appropriations subcommittees and two substantive legislative committees in each house—that handle tobacco legislation and related appropriations; and certain officials within the Department of Agriculture who were involved with the various tobacco programs of that department. This was a small group of people well known to each other and knowledgeable about all aspects of the tobacco industry and its relationship with the government.

[2] For a general discussion and introduction to the various techniques of systematic analysis, see Oran R. Young, *Systems of Political Science* (Englewood Cliffs, N.J.: Prentice-Hall, 1968), especially pp. 13–27.

J. Leiper Freeman in *The Political Process* (New York: Random House, 1965) and Ernest Griffith, *Congress: Its Contemporary Role* (New York: New York University Press, 1961) use the subsystem concept in their general analysis of the political process.

As long as no one objected too loudly, the important and complex tobacco programs, like price supports and export promotion, were conducted without interference from those not included in this subsystem. There are hundreds of similar subsystems functioning in Washington that quietly and efficiently bridge the gap created by the constitutional separation of powers.[3]

When a change in the prevailing power configuration is desired, but those in the subsystem are unwilling to accommodate such demands, outsiders seeking the change attempt to mobilize the latent antagonisms inherent in institutions whose authority and responsibility are defined within a framework of constitutionally separated powers. The subsystems serve to reduce the conflict and competition that might exist within this framework. On the other hand, the latent conflict in a government of separated powers can be used to spawn controversies that might result in policy change.

Those who seek to change a policy controlled by a subsystem often use the policymaking powers of one institution of government to provoke a response and further action from another. A different committee of Congress or an agency of the bureaucracy might be persuaded to concern itself with the issue, which heretofore had been within the guarded domain of the subsystem. Perhaps an interest group or a powerful individual encourages other groups to use their political powers to challenge those who in in the past had succeeded in keeping the conflict within manageable bounds. One agency of the bureaucracy might challenge the jurisdiction of another. All of these actions could receive further impetus by direct appeals to public opinion. Conflict is thus created and expanded as more and different actors are induced to challenge the decision makers in the subsystem.

Once control begins to pass from the traditional decision makers, it is difficult to predict what new directions policy will take. The only safe prediction is that there will be a struggle and a

[3] See Douglass Cater, *Power in Washington* (New York: Random House, 1964).

challenge to those who were in charge.[4] While the struggle goes on—
it can last for years—it is difficult to say *who* controls *what* in the
policy area affected. It becomes easier to bring about change while
the subsystem is in a state of disarray. Eventually things settle down
and a new subsystem emerges. Often it is different in terms of size
and membership from the one that existed when the controversy
started. The success of the challenge can sometimes be measured by
the permanence of any realignment that might occur within a subsystem.

TOBACCO POWER

Any challenge to the tobacco subsystem was fraught at the out-
set with serious difficulties. Long before the health warning was
threatened, tobacco power had established itself as an important
force in American politics. The tobacco coalition directly includes
growers, manufacturers, and distributors, and indirectly includes a
clientele of millions who smoke more than $14 billion worth of
tobacco products annually. The recipients of those $14 billion in-
clude manufacturers, advertising agencies, the mass media, farmers,
shopkeepers, and tax collectors. They work hard to discourage any
government activity that might in turn discourage the smoker.
Smokers dislike being told, particularly by politicians, that their
pleasures could be injurious to their health. Consequently, health-
oriented politicians are likely to devote their time to more popular
activities.

The tobacco interests find support in the American ethic because attempts to regulate business enterprise are generally received
by most Americans without enthusiasm and frequently with considerable suspicion. Often there is considerable disagreement within

4 For theoretical accounts of conflict theories of change, see E. E. Schattschneider, *The Semi-Sovereign People* (New York: Holt, Rinehart and Winston,
1960); Georg Simmel, *Conflict and the Web of Group-Affiliations* (New York:
Free Press, 1955); and Lewis Coser, *The Functions of Social Conflict* (New York:
Free Press, 1956).

the business community as to what business should be regulated. One industry will frequently ask the government to regulate a competitor. Yet, when the government does move to comprehensively regulate something considered basic, such as advertising, there is usually cohesive and rapid action to form a common defense.

Making the research findings of scientists available to the public through government action was a difficult task under these circumstances. The legions of tobacco supporters did all they could to make certain that smokers heeded the titillation of full color advertisements rather than the dark foreboding of the scientific community. Scientists, and those interested in bringing to the public information that would discourage smoking, had unsuccessfully challenged the pro-tobacco forces for many years.

NICOTIANA:
THE BEGINNINGS OF THE CONTROVERSY

The scientists' troubles began when a Frenchman introduced the native American plant, tobacco, to the world. Jean Nicot, the French ambassador to Portugal, wrote to a friend in 1560 that an American herb he had acquired had marvelous curative powers. Consumption of tobacco quickly gained popularity and Nicot earned a place for himself in history. His name became the base for the scientific term for tobacco, *Nicotiana*.

Shortly after Nicot made his discovery, skepticism of the marvelous curative powers of tobacco began to develop. Some condemned smoking as a foul, smelly habit that rendered social intercourse distasteful. More serious criticism developed in the 1850s when scientific evidence began to appear that supported the skeptics who questioned the medicinal value of cigarettes.

A British medical journal, *The Lancet,* published an article on March 14, 1857, that proved to have an element of timelessness about it. The scientists' indictment, which could well be the same today, read:

Tobacco is said to act on the mind by producing inactivity thereof; inability to think; drowsiness; irritability. . . . On the respiratory organs, it acts by causing consumption, haemoptysis, and inflammatory condition of the mucous membrane of the larynx, trachea, and bronchae, ulceration of the larynx; short irritable cough; hurried breathing. The circulating organs are affected by irritable heart circulation.[5]

These rather alarming charges against smoking received little public notice. There were relatively few smokers and chewers of tobacco in those days, so the medical disclosures were not interpreted as a major threat to the public health. Smoking was neither easy nor feminine because one had to roll his own or smoke a pipe or cigar. The introduction of the cigarette and the advertising that accompanied it in the early 1900s helped to remove these barriers.

The cigarette became popular very quickly, and smoking came to be a mark of social distinction. Spurred by advertising, which made cigarette smoking seem like good sense, and even healthful, sales soared.[6] Per capita annual consumption of cigarettes for people over 18 years old grew from 49 cigarettes in 1900 to over 4,100 by the early 1970s. This is more than 11 cigarettes per day for every American over the age of 18.

Small groups of social reformers, including advocates of the Prohibition Amendment, mounted a brief attack on cigarettes in the years prior to World War I. Their effort was short lived and unsuccessful. Using a strategy parallel to the prohibitionists', they attempted to secure anticigarette laws in nine southern and western states by 1913. The tide in favor of smoking, spurred by increased

[5] Quoted in a speech by Franklin B. Dryden, Assistant to the President, The Tobacco Institute Inc., before the 21st Tobacco Workers Conference, January 17–20, 1967, Williamsburg, Virginia (mimeo.).

[6] The advertisement that showed a plump damsel of 1920s vintage reaching for a Lucky instead of a sweet conveyed an important message to young ladies in various stages of obesity. This ad is credited with making smoking acceptable to women. Medical doctors, athletes, and movie stars, tempted by large fees, gladly signed testimonials that implied that their good health and looks and, in the case of the doctors, those of their patients, were in no way compromised by smoking.

advertising, the political emancipation of women, and social practices such as illegal liquor consumption, was so strong that by 1929 the tide for state legislation to prohibit cigarette consumption by adults had receded.[7]

Cigarette sales increased every year until 1953 when newspapers publicized a report given at a dental society meeting in New York City associating cigarette smoking with lung cancer. The sales scare lasted only two years. After this trauma, sales rose each year without interruption until 1964 when there was another slight, temporary drop after the Surgeon General issued his report, *Smoking and Health*. During the next two years, per capita consumption increased slightly. From 1966 through 1971, it decreased to less than 4,000 cigarettes per year.

A CHALLENGE TO THE SUBSYSTEM

For nearly 45 years the question of what the government should do about warning the cigarette consumer has been on the agenda of one governmental institution or another. Those who opposed a warning were able to keep it a low priority item for 35 of those 45 years. The tobacco interests were successful in keeping the issue within the confines of a few agencies and within the offices and committee rooms of a few key congressmen. No one could gather enough support to bring about any change in the status quo. Those who favored a cigarette health warning had to devise some method to involve other agencies and different members of Congress, to interest them in working for the adoption of legislation that would limit cigarette consumption. Until early in the 1960s, the health interests were unsuccessful in doing this.

The strategy of the cigarette interests was to play off various agencies of the bureaucracy against each other or against Congress to prevent the smoking and health controversy from expanding.

[7] Andrew Sinclair, *The Era of Excess* (New York: Harper & Row, 1964), pp. 180–181.

This style of tobacco politics resulted in little government regulation of tobacco advertising or sales. The strategy was successful as long as there was little public support for a government policy to reduce cigarette consumption. As scientific evidence began to document the link between smoking and ill health, pressure for regulation grew, but the tobacco subsystem proved impenetrable to these demands. Tobacco was more firmly entrenched and more richly supported than most other consumer products. One journalist succinctly described the dilemma of the health groups: "If tobacco were spinach the government would have outlawed it years ago, and no one would have given a damn." [8] There were, however, many who cared.

The government proposed that a health warning be given in advertising as well as on cigarette packages. Such a statement in advertising, in all likelihood, would have been more effective than the package warning alone. This threat to advertising encouraged others to join the tobacco people in opposition. The American Newspaper Publishers Association, the Advertising Federation of America, the Association of National Advertisers, the Radio Advertising Bureau, and the National Association of Broadcasters, all fearing that advertising restrictions would mean a loss of revenues, aligned themselves with the tobacco interests. This coalition strengthened the position of those who supported the business-as-usual tobacco-government decision-making structure.

Because the tobacco interests exerted considerable influence within the traditional legislative system through congressmen serving on committees or subcommittees immediately involved in tobacco politics, there was little hope for the successful initiation of new policy within Congress. To effect a change in public policy, other avenues of policymaking had to be used. Through the collaboration of a few members of Congress and two agencies of the bureaucracy that were not part of the tobacco subsystem, a new coalition was formed to combat the tobacco interests. Congress was

[8] D. S. Greenberg, "Cigarettes and Cancer: Pressure Grows for the Government to Respond to a Health Hazard," *Science*, May 18, 1962, p. 838.

generally unfriendly to consumer legislation, since consumers rarely generated pressures or did favors on a scale to match the organized interest groups. As consumer groups organized in the late 1960s, congressional resistance to consumer legislation lessened. When the controversy began, however, the fate of the cigarette health warning, like other consumer measures, depended heavily on the power of administrative agencies to make public policy.

ADMINISTRATIVE POLICYMAKING

Over the years, Congress has found it necessary to grant or delegate policymaking powers to administrative agencies because insurmountable obstacles face Congress in writing legislation with sufficient detail and foresight to meet all of the situations that might arise under that legislation. Recognizing this difficulty, Congress leaves it to the agencies to initiate policies and promulgate rules and regulations to implement the broad programs created by legislation.

Frequently Congress gives only the sketchiest guidelines to the bureaucracy, often requiring an agency to run a program in "the public interest" or in "the public interest, convenience, and necessity." These guidelines give agencies considerable freedom in administrative rulemaking. The power that agencies have been delegated over the past several decades has made them an important force in the public policy process; some have even called them a fourth branch of government. Agency policy, made in the form of rules, regulations, and interpretations of the way a law is to be applied, accounts for most of the policy output of governments today. The largest number of policies that directly affect and govern people and property are made by administrative agencies through powers delegated by Congress.

Agency policymaking powers result in regulations having the effect of law—no different from the end product of the congressional legislative process or the decisions of courts of law. In fact, agencies are capable of adopting regulations under delegated authority that Congress itself might not have adopted.[9] This is often the case when strong lobbies prevent elected members of legislatures from responding to public demands. While Congress was struggling to strengthen gun control legislation in the wake of the murder of Senator Robert F. Kennedy, the Post Office Department used its delegated authority to discourage the shipment of all guns through the mails. The National Rifle Association had succeeded for years in keeping Congress inactive, but it was taken by surprise by the swift action of the Postmaster General.[10]

The issuance of a requirement that there be a health warning in cigarette advertising and on packages was also the work of an administrative agency in the face of anticipated congressional inaction. The Federal Trade Commission first proposed the rule requiring a health warning and later felt the full wrath of congressional disapproval. Congress would not have done what the commission did. The commission rule called for a warning in advertising and on packages. Congress wanted neither, but the commission's action forced Congress to accept first half, then all of the ruling. Congress accepted the label on packages reluctantly and coupled it with a severe rebuke to the FTC. This rebuke of the FTC is a clear example of how Congress can control the authority it delegates to administrative agencies. More important than the initial actions of the FTC or the congressional rebuke that followed them is the fact that the commission started a process that eventually brought about substantial policy change. In this instance, agency policymaking powers broke the stalemate perpetuated by subsystem politics and opened the way for a series of changes in policy affecting cigarette smoking and public health.

[9] Similarly, an executive agency might administer an act in such a way as to transform the original legislative intent of Congress into another kind of substantive policy. See David S. McLellan and Donald Clare, "Public Law 480: The Metamorphosis of a Law," *Eagleton Institute Cases in Practical Politics* (New York: McGraw-Hill, 1965).

[10] The new regulation requires that all packages containing guns be marked "firearms" and local police notified of their arrival before they leave the post office for delivery. *The Washington Post,* June 13, 1968. See: 33 *Federal Register,* pp. 8667 and 8678 (1968).

The importance of the bureaucracy as a policymaking institution raises some basic questions for democratic government. This is not the place to define in detail the complicated and elusive ideals of democracy. Any definition, however, would include at least these elements: a democratic government provides means through which citizens can participate in policymaking, and it also provides machinery citizens can use to hold the government accountable for the decisions it makes. An independent judiciary and frequent elections based on a wide franchise help to insure that these conditions will be met. When policymaking powers are concentrated within an agency of nonelected bureaucrats, the effectiveness of both of the above may be lessened. It is difficult, although far from impossible, to build both accountability and participation into the policymaking process when administrative agencies are the chief policymakers.[11]

In the cigarette labeling controversy, the legality and propriety of allowing the FTC to require and enforce a health warning on cigarettes were questioned. The commission was accused of acting unconstitutionally, in isolation from any checks generated by a system of constitutionally separated powers. Although one should not assume that the powers of administrative agencies are always "natural and good," as one student of politics recently warned,[12] the dangers of excessive and arbitrary use of those powers are reduced when the agency acts as a part of a system in which power is widely dispersed. During the course of the controversy, it became clear that the FTC was not acting in isolation. On the contrary, there were checks on the commission's powers through its interaction and conflict with other agencies, the public, interest groups, the courts, and eventually Congress. This indicates that interests broader than those represented solely by the bureaucracy were

[11] See William W. Boyer, *Bureaucracy on Trial: Policy Making by Government Agencies* (Indianapolis: Bobbs-Merrill, 1964) and Peter Woll, *American Bureaucracy* (New York: Norton, 1967) on this point and for a general discussion of agency policymaking powers.
[12] Theodore J. Lowi, *The End of Liberalism: Ideology, Policy, and the Crisis of Public Authority* (New York: Norton, 1969), p. 155.

represented in the policymaking process. It was the existence of agency powers that gave the impetus for policy change and innovation in this case. Power concentrated in the hands of possessive congressional committees was forced out into the open where it had to be shared because bureaucratic agencies had the authority to act.

BUREAUCRATS AND CONGRESSMEN

The cigarette labeling controversy demonstrated that the bureaucracy acting alone could not be successful in its policymaking activities. In the labeling fight, as in other areas of domestic policymaking, the bureaucracy found it difficult to start anything without at least the acquiescence and usually the outright support of members of Congress and portions of the interested public. Congressmen, bureaucrats, and pressure groups each have at least one political resource the other needs. The bureaucracy has expertise and knowledge derived from continued experience. Congressmen control the money and are closer to the political power bureaucrats lack. Pressure groups often are the catalytic agents and possess the power to unite congressmen and bureaucrats for action.

These rather fundamental relationships are often overlooked by those who argue that bureaucratic policymaking power is excessive in that it is responsible for the origination of most major legislation. In a strict technical sense this might be true. Often the idea for a new piece of legislation, or at least its impetus, comes from within the halls of Congress instead of the monotonous corridors of the bureaucracy. A member of Congress finds it easy to give voice to a new idea. He can do it alone or with the assistance of his personal staff. An idea planted in the ear of a staff man can be put into formal legislative language by other congressional staff offices in a few days.[13] The member then drops the bill in the hopper and,

[13] In addition to legislative draftsmen who work within some congressmen's offices and committee counsels, each house of Congress has an Office of the Legislative Counsel. This office will, upon presentation of only vague and minimal ideas, draft a bill for a member of Congress.

if he is really interested in pressing for action, he might make a speech on the floor or take other steps to gain public support.

Thousands of bills are introduced each year, but only a few become law. The low productivity rate is a reflection of the inability of most members to successfully guide legislation through Congress.[14] Power in Congress is concentrated in a few hands. Committee chairmen hold nearly complete control over the bills that come within their committees' jurisdictions. If a member wants to enact a bill, he needs the support of the appropriate chairman. It is often difficult to enlist this support from within Congress. Consequently, the eager member faced with a disinterested committee chairman must look outside Congress for the help he needs to enact his bill. The congressman has the option of turning to the bureaucracy for expertise and, perhaps, presidential support, and to a pressure group for necessary public support.[15]

The bureaucrat's problems are nearly the opposite of the congressman's. Most bureaucrats find it difficult to initiate change, particularly if that change is substantial and unwanted by the leaders of a powerful subsystem. The bureaucrat has no readily available public forum, and his ideas have to be cleared by bureaucratic committees in and outside of his agency. The Office of Management and Budget has to clear the new policy to make certain it conforms with the president's program. All of this is complicated; it takes time, and issues tend to die because of these difficult procedures. A member of Congress has access to the public, the White House, and the cabinet. Drawing on these assets, he can assist the agency by shortening the bureaucrat's clearance process and by removing some opposition. There is a system of mutual dependencies even at the stage of policy initiation, and these dependencies are observable right through the implementation stage.

Tobacco politics would have continued as it had for years if

14 Often members introduce bills for constituents as a favor. Members generally don't expect to see these bills enacted; usually they are introduced with the understanding that they will be ignored.

15 See Clem Miller, *Member of the House* (New York: Scribner, 1962), pp. 143–160.

those favoring change had relied solely on Congress or solely on the bureaucracy to initiate that change. Instead, congressmen and bureaucrats in league with some interest groups called on each other for help. The bureaucracy had a long, although mixed, history of concern with the content of cigarette advertising and the dangers of smoking to health. In its employ were scientists and economists who had devoted a large portion of their professional careers to these issues. At least one agency in the bureaucracy, the Federal Trade Commission, had been ready to implement a health warning for several years but lacked the power or support to do so. To realize their goals, bureaucrats had to act in league with members of Congress and special interest representatives. Once the coalition was formed and active, the tobacco subsystem began to quake.

2

SMOKING AND
ADMINISTRATIVE POLITICS

When medical research began to establish a positive relationship
between illness and smoking early in the 1900s, the cigarette controversy began to move slowly toward the center of the political arena.
At the dawn of the century, the effects of smoking on health had
generated controversy only in the medical community. The cigarette
health issue did not begin to concern the public or the government
until the 1950s. The normal difficulties of transferring matters of
scientific importance to the lay public were exacerbated by the
efforts of the cigarette manufacturers to allay any fears smokers
might have been experiencing as a result of conflict in the medical
field. When unfavorable research findings were released, the manufacturers found ways to discredit and obliterate them in the public

consciousness through more glamorous advertisements and intensified lobbying. Each major medical discovery and government response was followed by a reaction of the manufacturers or their advertisers. An examination of the chronology in the Appendix reveals
this pattern of action and reaction in tobacco politics.

Results of the first major health study were released in 1939.
They received little public consideration, but what little attention
they did receive began to teach cigarette makers how to cope with
future health scares. The early health studies failed to gain much
credence because they dealt only with the medical *records* of human
beings and not with human beings themselves. These studies were
prepared from data contained in personal medical and mortality
records of large groups of people. Over the years the significance of
the studies has grown. The studies indicate that more cigarette
smokers contract lung cancer than nonsmokers. Furthermore, they
demonstrate that symptoms like chronic cough, sputum production,
breathlessness, chest illness, and decreased lung function are found
more often in smokers than in nonsmokers.

RESEARCH UNCOVERS A HEALTH HAZARD

As frightening as the results of the earlier studies were, they
failed to make the impact on the public that the post-1954 studies
did. These studies dealt with smokers and nonsmokers, were conducted in laboratories and hospitals, and included autopsies. The
results of the first of these studies, by E. Cuyler Hammond and
Daniel Horn, concluded firmly that smoking causes lung cancer.[1]
Later research discovered major and disturbing changes in the cellu-
lar structure of smokers' lungs. The statistics were startling: they revealed that 93.2 percent of smokers had abnormal lung cells, whereas
only 1.2 percent of the lungs of nonsmokers contained evidence of
abnormality. The Public Health Service analyzed seven population

---

[1] E. Cuyler Hammond and Daniel Horn, "The Relationship Between Human Smoking Habits and Death Rates: A Follow-Up Study of 187,766 Men,"
Journal of the American Medical Association, August 7, 1954.

studies ten years after the first study was released. It was found that among 1,123,000 men, the death rate for smokers was nearly 70 percent higher than the death rate for nonsmokers.[2] Hundreds of studies have been conducted since 1954, nearly all of them expanding the catalog of chronic diseases attributable to cigarette smoking. Besides cancer of a wide variety of organs, the list now includes heart diseases and diseases of the respiratory system. Drs. Hammond and Horn have written that the death rate from all causes for male smokers between the ages of 45 and 64 is twice as high as that for nonsmokers.

Research conducted after 1954 gave public health groups the impetus to mobilize their educational and lobbying activities. The Public Health Cancer Association and the American Cancer Society adopted resolutions acknowledging support of the 1954 studies and agreeing that there is a positive relationship between smoking and lung cancer. A report issued simultaneously by the British Ministry of Health came to the same conclusion. Four public health groups in 1957 joined to study the accumulating scientific evidence. The conclusion of their survey, released on March 6 of that year, stated:

> The sum total of scientific evidence establishes beyond reasonable doubt that cigarette smoking is a causative factor in the rapidly increasing incidence of human epidermoid carcinoma of the lung. *The evidence of a cause-effect relationship is adequate for the initiation of public health measures.* [Emphasis added] [3]

The magnitude of the cigarette smoking problem for public health and the national welfare is enormous. Deaths from lung cancer and heart diseases are reaching epidemic proportions. In 40 years, deaths from lung cancer have increased from 2,500 each

---

[2] U.S. Department of Health, Education and Welfare, *Smoking and Health: Report of the Advisory Committee to the Surgeon General of the Public Health Service,* Public Health Service Document No. 1103 (Washington, D.C.: U.S. Government Printing Office, 1964), p. 28.

[3] The four groups were the American Cancer Society, the National Cancer Institute, the American Heart Association, and the National Heart Institute.

year to about 60,000. It has been estimated that 4,000 teenagers take up smoking *each day* and that continuation of that rate would result in 1,000,000 youngsters now in school dying of lung cancer before they reached the age of 70. The 45 million American smokers constitute a large portion of the national population. Their care, cure, and skill replacement in economic terms alone is staggering. The present attitude of the Public Health Service was very well summarized by Dr. William H. Stewart, the Surgeon General, at the World Conference on Smoking and Health in September 1967:

> The proposition that cigarette smoking is hazardous to human health long ago passed the realm of possibility. It has now gone beyond the probable, to the point of demonstrable fact. . . . The sentence with which all of us are familiar—"Caution: Cigarette Smoking May Be Hazardous To Your Health"—is inadequate as a description of the present state of our knowledge. Cigarette smoking *is* hazardous to health. . . . This is no longer a matter of opinion nor an evangelical slogan. It is a flat scientific fact.[4]

INDUSTRY'S RESPONSE

The tobacco industry is quick to point to the major shortcomings of scientific research on cigarette smoking. Their arguments are both effective and, to some extent, well founded. All of the unfavorable cigarette findings released to date use statistical evidence in an attempt to establish a link between smoking and disease. Statistical correlations show that those who smoke contract a variety of respiratory and related diseases at greater rates than those who do not. Thus far, scientists have been unable to determine exactly which of the hundreds of substances in cigarettes causes diseases. Any statistician will admit that any two items might be correlated, but the fact of correlation does not establish any causal relationship. The statistical correlation between smoking and disease could be

---

4 Quoted in: Warren G. Magnuson and Jean Carper, *The Dark Side of the Market Place* (Englewood Cliffs, New Jersey: Prentice-Hall, 1968), p. 188.

purely chance. Fluctuations in the stock markets have been correlated with sun spot activity. Does this mean that sun spots cause
the stock markets to fluctuate, or vice versa? Probably not. The
statistics used to relate smoking to ill health are open to similar
criticism, according to the tobacco groups and their allies. Perhaps
the illnesses of smokers are related to something other than cigarette
smoking, they say. It is conceivable that nonsmokers are self-protec-
tive in their life patterns. Their interest in self-protection could
account for their longevity. Cigarette smoking could have very little
to do with it. Nonsmokers might live longer because they watch
their weight and diet more carefully than the smoker who leads a
more "reckless life." The industry has advanced the idea that
environmental studies need to be made to understand if so-called
cigarette-related diseases are not instead related to environmental
factors.[5]

Medical research is endeavoring to isolate the harmful ingredients in cigarettes and cigarette smoke. Since there are over
1,000 components in cigarette smoke, the task of isolating those
that inflict harm on humans is exceedingly difficult. Some research
blames the tar or nicotine content of tobacco; others the cheaper
tobaccos used in modern filter cigarettes. Still others feel that certain chemicals added to cigarette tobacco are responsible. Perhaps
it is the wrapping paper on the tobacco. Newer theories hold that
within the bodies of certain individuals there is some matter that
when mixed with cigarette smoke causes cancer. If that matter could
be isolated, it might be possible for the smoker to immunize himself against the ill effects of smoking.

The absence of specific information on those ingredients in
cigarettes that cause diseases is not viewed by most scientists as
disproving the relationship between smoking and ill health. They
claim their evidence results in an overwhelming indictment of
cigarette smoking. Since scientists do not believe that people will
give up smoking, discovery of a harmless cigarette is consequently of

[5] A well-written summary of the tobacco position by Robert C. Hockett,
associate scientific director of the Tobacco Industry Research Committee, appears in the April, 1964 issue of the *Yale Scientific Magazine.*

considerable concern to both the scientific and cigarette-producing communities. The task that seems most immediate to the largest portion of the health community, however, is to communicate to the public the message that smoking is a threat to health.

The case against smoking has grown stronger in recent years. And the manufacturers' argument about the invalidity of statistical evidence impresses fewer people as medical evidence continues to accumulate. Commissioner Philip Elman of the Federal Trade Commission reacted to the increasing scientific evidence this way in the commission's June 1967 report to Congress:

> I regret that the Commission has not also recommended to the Congress that (1) cigarette advertising be banned entirely on television and radio, and (2) the "super-king-size" 100-mm. cigarettes, now being extensively promoted by the industry, be banned from interstate commerce as too dangerous for human consumption.

BIRTH OF A LOBBY

The tobacco men began to react somewhat differently to research findings after the results of the 1954 studies were announced. The first visible sign of significant change was the creation of the Tobacco Industry Research Committee (now called the Council for Tobacco Research—U.S.A.). Its purpose is to distribute funds for scientific research for studies on the use of tobacco and its effect on health. In an active 18 years since its founding, $20 million in grants have been awarded to 260 individuals at 192 research institutions throughout the United States.[6]

The creation of this research organization was an indication

---

6 In addition to the $20 million expended by the council, the six major cigarette producers contributed $18 million since 1964 to the American Medical Association Education and Research Foundation. The initial award came at the time the Federal Trade Commission announced that it was considering a health warning requirement. The American Medical Association was not active in support of the FTC's proposal.

that there would be intensified opposition from the tobacco interests on the health issue. Whenever criticism of smoking grew, the tobacco interests responded by more research or more public relations expenditures. The Tobacco Institute, Inc., a lobbying public relations group formed in 1958, was a further indication of the industry's will to contain the possible adverse political effects of the health studies. In 1964, cigarette producers set up still another organization called the Cigarette Advertising Code, Inc. This was a self-policing organization to assure fairness and accuracy in competitive advertising.

The most important of these organizations as far as the cigarette labeling controversy is concerned is the Tobacco Institute. Fourteen of the major tobacco producers formed the institute, and the presidents of the companies sit on its board. It is financed by contributions from these large corporations, which contribute according to their share of the market.

In its promotional literature, the institute notes that it is concerned with the historical role of tobacco, its place in the economy, and public understanding of the tobacco industry. To these ends, it publishes two small periodicals, *The Tobacco News* and *Tobacco And Health Research*. The real genius of the institute rests with the executives it hires. Former Ambassador George V. Allen was at one time director of the institute. A well-known and highly regarded career diplomat, Ambassador Allen brought considerable prestige to the organization. When the ambassador returned to government service as Director of the Foreign Service Institute in 1966, the tobacco men were successful in hiring former Senator Earle C. Clements as their director. For two years prior to that, the former senator was a lobbyist for the six major cigarette companies.

Clements brought a very impressive set of credentials to the Tobacco Institute, including a public service record of long standing and a political record that few could equal. Previously, he had been Kentucky's governor and represented that state in the House and the Senate. With the loss of his Senate seat, he eventually returned to Kentucky where he became state highway commissioner. As an alumnus of Congress he still had floor privileges, though he was never known to have used them during the debates on the labeling bill. Indebted to political interests in Kentucky, his services as a lobbyist for all the deep-South tobacco interests were not difficult to obtain.

Politically, Clements was as close to the Johnson administration as anyone could possibly have been. In 1951, as the junior senator from Kentucky, Clements was placed on the powerful Senate Democratic Policy Committee at the urging of Lyndon Johnson when the death of Virgil Chapman, senior senator from Kentucky, left a seat open. Clements reciprocated in 1953 by endorsing Johnson for the position of minority leader, giving the impression, since Clements had established himself as a liberal, that the conservative Johnson was acceptable to all quarters of the party. Under Johnson's leadership, the Senate Democrats accepted Clements as minority whip and later as majority whip. During Johnson's absence because of a heart attack in 1955, Clements was entrusted with the rank and power of acting majority leader. A year later Majority Leader Johnson, knowing full well the consequences for Clements, asked him to vote in the affirmative on the medicare bill, a vote that contributed to his defeat in Kentucky.[7] Again Johnson came to the rescue of his old friend and secured for him the position of executive director of the Senate Democratic Campaign Fund. One of Clements's last activities for Lyndon B. Johnson came in 1960 when, as an advance man for Johnson, he attempted to gather delegate support for the majority leader after it became clear that Senator Hubert Humphrey's campaign for president had collapsed. In addition to this long personal involvement with Johnson, Clements claimed a rather unique tie to the White House. His daughter, Bess Abell, served as Lady Bird Johnson's social secretary. As a Johnson crony and working with the best known law partner of the firm of Arnold, Fortas and Porter—Abe Fortas, a Johnson confidant and later a Supreme Court Justice and one-time nominee for the Chief Justice position—Clements helped plan and execute a careful and forceful campaign

---

[7] See Rowland Evans and Robert Novak, *Lyndon B. Johnson: The Exercise of Power* (New York: New American Library, 1966), p. 159ff.

to save the tobacco industry from any governmental action that might be harmful to its sales.

The government action that the cigarette manufacturers anticipated as early as 1954 did not begin to materialize until the mid-1960s. The slowness of the government's response to the smoking studies of the 1950s was due, in part, to the successful efforts of the Tobacco Institute and, in part, to the relative weakness of the public health interest groups. The institute had enough economic and political power to make certain that government activity would be unproductive. The disorganized array of health groups had neither the leadership nor the financial means to coalesce into an effective lobbying organization. They were overwhelmed by the giant tobacco industry and its supporters from the early 1950s onward.

TOBACCO IN THE ECONOMY

An index of the strength of tobacco power in politics is the size of the public expenditure on cigarette consumption. Smokers in the United States were spending over $7 billion for cigarettes in 1963, as the government started to consider the issuance of a health warning. This impressive sum was shared by widely disparate segments of the population. A portion of it went to 600,000 tobacco farm families in 26 states. Over 34,000 workers in cigarette factories earned some of the $7 billion. And the treasuries of national, state, and local governments were enriched by receipt of nearly $3.25 billion of this cigarette booty in excise and other taxes. According to the Tobacco Institute, cigarette taxes amounted to three times as much as the tobacco grower's total sales receipts for tobacco leaf.

The advertising industry, and through it the mass media, was in the cigarette selling business to the extent of $312 million a year in 1967. Cigarette promotions earned 8 percent of the total advertising revenue for television, 2.7 percent for radio, 2.3 percent for newspapers, and 3.3 percent for magazines. When these statistics are expanded by the expenditures on warehousing, shipping, and other related aspects of the cigarette business, it becomes clear that the manufacturing, distribution, and consumption of cigarettes are an enterprise that touches large numbers of people. Some are, of course, touched more than others.

Tobacco sales in the state of North Carolina accounted for nearly half of the total receipts from farm products. Kentucky, South Carolina, Virginia and, to a lesser extent, Georgia and Tennessee, also produced significant amounts of tobacco. These same states were leaders in cigarette production. Attempts to discourage tobacco consumption could have had important consequences in these states both economically and politically.

CONGRESS REBUFFS HEALTH PROPONENTS

Members of Congress from tobacco states were in powerful positions in the early 1960s. In the Senate nearly one-fourth of the committees were chaired by men from the six tobacco states. Of the 21 committees in the House, tobacco state congressmen chaired seven.[8] Given the power distribution in Congress, the members from these states could exert extraordinary influence on matters that would come before their committees. As committee chairmen they could demand the support of their colleagues in return for legislative favors covering the broad spectrum of congressional action. Chairmen could use this power skillfully to indefinitely delay consideration of measures which might adversely affect their constituents. The tobacco state members used their power to protect the tobacco industry.

Certain members of Congress had worked for years to introduce legislation that would have either restricted the sale of cigarettes or conveyed health warnings to the public. More than 15 bills were introduced in the House and Senate by various lawmakers between 1962 and 1964 alone. None of these were considered seriously. The

---

[8] Maurine B. Neuberger, *Smoke Screen: Tobacco and the Public Welfare* (Englewood Cliffs, New Jersey: Prentice-Hall, 1963), p. 110.

absence of public support for these health measures, combined with the opposition of the tobacco congressmen, prevented such proposals from receiving serious consideration.

The first committee hearings concerning smoking and health were conducted in 1957 by John A. Blatnik (D.–Minnesota) who was chairman of the Legal and Monetary Affairs Subcommittee of the Government Operations Committee. The purpose of those hearings was to define or redefine the responsibility of the Federal Trade Commission for enforcing standards of truthfulness in advertising claims relating to the effectiveness of cigarette filters. Blatnik confessed during the hearings that his physician had warned him about his smoking habit but, despite the warning, he continued to smoke cigarettes and enjoy them. His personal testimonial on the enjoyment of smoking, however, did not assuage the anger of the tobacco interests over the content of the subcommittee's report. The report concluded, "The cigarette manufacturers have deceived the American public through their advertising of cigarettes." The subcommittee found that an individual was not safer if he elected to smoke filter tip cigarettes. Filters were not as effective as the manufacturers claimed; furthermore, lower grade tobacco can be used in filter cigarettes and lower grade leaf contains more tars and nicotine. Shortly after the report was issued, Blatnik's subcommittee was dissolved and he lost his chairmanship. The subcommittee has since been revived, but Blatnik is no longer a member of it. His absence has been attributed to the power of the tobacco lobby.[9]

While the friends of tobacco had successfully prevented meaningful congressional action on the health issue, the antismoking interests began concentrating their efforts elsewhere. There are

[9] Abolishing a subcommitte of the Government Operations Committee for punitive reasons has happened more than once. The Subcommittee on Foreign Operations and Government Information was threatened with abolition by the chairman of the full committee, William L. Dawson (D.–Illinois), in the spring of 1968 because of its criticism of United States aid programs and the progress of land reform in Vietnam. *The Congressional Quarterly* staff reported that informal sources indicated the order was a case of the hawks about to devour the subcommittee. (*Congressional Quarterly Weekly Report*, No. 17, April 26, 1968, p. 914.)

several points in the policymaking system where policy determinations can be influenced. When those interested in a cigarette health
warning found they could not be effective in Congress, they intensified their efforts in the bureaucracy and in the courts.

SMOKERS SUE MANUFACTURERS

Cigarette manufacturers have been subjected to judicial proceedings by lung cancer victims or their survivors on approximately
70 separate occasions. The availability of scientific data that linked
smoking and lung cancer spurred cancer victims or their heirs to
sue, but many of the cases were initiated in the late 1940s and early
1950s, when the studies were not as definitive as they were later.
The arguments against the manufacturers rested in most instances
on the theory that cigarette producers acted in violation of their
responsibility to supply a product of merchantable quality. Attorneys for the smokers argued that manufacturers had an obligation
to make sure that cigarettes were healthful, and that manufacturers
had implied such assurance in promotional activities. Throughout
the 1950s and early 1960s, manufacturers of cigarettes were protected against suit, according to the courts, because they had no way
to foresee the harm their product might do to a consumer.[10] This
left open the question of what responsibility a producer might have
when medical studies more clearly, or even absolutely, showed that
smoking causes diseases. Then, of course, the harm could be fore-
seen.

One of the cases, brought by Edward L. Green of Miami in
1957, caused considerable difficulty to the cigarette companies. Mr.
Green started to smoke Lucky Strikes when he was 16 years old in
1925. After smoking three packages a day, he discovered in 1956

10 See Richard A. Wegman, "Cigarettes and Health: A Legal Analysis," 51
Cornell Law Quarterly, 678 (1966), for a detailed analysis of many of the suits
brought against cigarette manufacturers.

that he had contracted lung cancer. He commenced an action against the American Tobacco Company in 1957 that was continued by his son in 1958 after the elder Mr. Green's death and resulted in a jury verdict for the company. A United States Court of Appeals affirmed the judgment.[11]

Although the company won on the first round, Mr. Green's heirs succeeded in having another court of appeals direct a new trial. This time the court directed a new jury to consider the question of whether the American Tobacco Company's cigarettes were reasonably fit for general public consumption. The new jury found that cigarettes were reasonably safe and wholesome, and Mr. Green's heirs were denied at that time any part of the $1.5 million they sought.

The medical evidence introduced at the trial did have some impact on the jury. The foreman of the jury at Mr. Green's trial was a pack-a-day smoker who, after listening to the medical evidence, gave up smoking halfway through the trial. He explained afterwards that if the judge had asked the jury members to decide whether or not cigarettes were safe, they would have said no. The judge had instead asked them to decide if cigarettes were reasonably safe and wholesome for human consumption. The key word was "reasonably." The jury apparently decided that if it took cigarettes 20 to 30 years to affect Mr. Green, they were reasonably safe.[12]

The decision was appealed three years later because of subsequent Florida court decisions concerning liability. This time, in light of the new decisions, the court decided in favor of Mr. Green. The decision read in part:

> We are now left in no substantial doubt that under Florida law the decedent was entitled to rely on the implied assurance that the Lucky Strike cigarettes were wholesome and fit for the purpose intended and that under the facts found by the jury his personal representative and widow are entitled to hold the manufacturers absolutely liable for

11 *Green v. American Tobacco Co.* 304 F 2d 70 (5th cir. 1962).
12 *The New York Times,* November 30, 1964, p. 1.

the injuries already found by a prior jury to have been sustained by him.[13]

This decision, favorable to the descendants of lung cancer victims, did not stand. The full court of appeals, in April 1969, reversed the decision and held that the American Tobacco Company was not liable for Mr. Green's death from lung cancer. Even if the earlier decision had stood, it probably would not have opened the floodgates against cigarette manufacturers. One of the unanticipated bonuses for the manufacturers of the new package label is that the health warning will make it more difficult, if not impossible, for anyone to sue for breach of warranty. The consumer of cigarettes has been warned by the manufacturer and by health groups through the mass media. One now smokes at his own risk; the manufacturers have relieved themselves of a major part of their responsibility under the law of liability. It can no longer be claimed that the manufacturer implies his product is entirely harmless. But if scientists should discover one or a number of ingredients in cigarettes that cause disease and manufacturers do not remove these ingredients, chances are that someone could successfully win a suit even though there is a warning on packages.

BUREAUCRATIC CONFLICT

While the courts and Congress experienced procedural and political difficulties with the cigarette health issue that were peculiar to those institutions, the bureaucracy was experiencing some of its own. A gigantic, complex operation, the bureaucracy employs about two and one-half million people in hundreds of agencies. One agency or another has had some interest in cigarettes since the turn of the century. There has, however, been little agreement among them on what the government position is, or what it should be, concerning smoking and health. The cigarette issue divided the

---

[13] Quoted in *The New York Times,* January 27, 1968.

bureaucracy rather sharply, pointing out the inescapable fact that although the bureaucracy is huge, it is anything but monolithic in its views. On cigarettes, agencies were on both ends of the policy spectrum. Some were attempting to boost cigarette and tobacco sales, while others were planning and operating programs designed to reduce cigarette consumption.

The United States Department of Agriculture's (USDA) interest in tobacco is related to its mission as the protector of the farmer and the promoter of his products. According to then Senator Maurine Neuberger (D.–Oregon), officials of the department's Tobacco Division once disparagingly referred to the cigarette-health crusade as a big smokescreen. The department administers price support programs for tobacco and endeavors to promote the sales of U.S. tobacco abroad. At the height of the smoking and health controversy, the Department of Agriculture was distributing an expensive sales promotion film that it had paid to have produced. The film stressed the virtues of cigarette smoking, and it was available at no charge to any nation that wanted to consider importing U.S. tobacco products.

Former Secretary of Agriculture Orville Freeman found himself in a tight spot when reporters questioned him about the continuation of tobacco price supports in view of recent smoking and health revelations. In what could be a political classic, the secretary responded that the government could in good conscience continue price supports and, indeed, must continue the price support program for tobacco. If the program were discontinued, he argued, tobacco prices would fall and cigarettes would cost less. The price reduction would then result in more people smoking and this, after all, would be contrary to the spirit of the health studies.

Later the Department of Agriculture took an official position against the inclusion of a health warning on packages or in advertising. Acting to protect their constituent tobacco producers, the department wrote:

Much more explicit identifications of the constituents of tobacco smoke and more complete understanding of their role as related to

it be sought and achieved. Only this will provide an ade-
for deciding whether or not such stringent provisions as
in [the bill, which required only the health warning on pack-
ages] are warranted.[14]

The views of the Department of Agriculture found little support in the Federal Trade Commission. While there were people
in the commission concerned with cigarette health questions, it
was the commission's jurisdiction over unfair and deceptive trade
practices that brought about their earliest regulation of cigarette
manufacturers. Since the early 1930s, the commission had brought
approximately 20 actions against cigarette companies for false or
misleading advertising. Many of these actions involved what the
commission considered misleading health claims. The manufacturers of Chesterfields were prohibited, for example, from claiming
their product had "no adverse effect upon the nose, throat or ac-
cessory organs." [15] Another producer was proscribed from claiming
that Kools would keep one's head clear in winter or any other time,
give extra protection, or provide an excellent safeguard during cold
months.[16]

The commission broadened its attack on cigarette advertising
in September 1955, when it adopted some advertising guides. It
prohibited, among other things, stating or implying in advertising
that there is medical approval of cigarette smoking in general or
smoking any brand of cigarette in particular.

After the guides were issued, the Federal Trade Commission
attempted to monitor cigarette advertising. Monitoring ads and
moving to prohibit some of them did not satisfy the commission's
goals, however. In the light of the increasing scientific data that
questioned the healthfulness of cigarette consumption, the actions

[14] Letter to Senator Warren G. Magnuson, printed in *Cigarette Labeling and
Advertising, Hearings Before The Committee on Commerce, United States Senate,*
89th Congress, 1st Session, 1965, p. 28.
[15] *Liggett and Myers Tobacco Co.,* 55 Federal Trade Commission 354 (1958).
[16] *Brown and Williamson Tobacco Corporation,* 34 Federal Trade Commission 1689 (1942).

of the commission looked puny and insignificant. The commission knew that consumption of cigarettes was increasing rapidly, particularly among younger age groups.[17] It attributed this increase to advertising that portrayed smoking in an attractive way, particularly on television. Advertisements quite naturally dwell only on whatever satisfactions there might be in smoking. They associate smoking with individuals or groups worthy of emulation, especially by the young. Smoking is portrayed as being fun, romantic, and even sexy.

To the FTC's consternation, these advertisements did not violate any law. They did not even violate the intent of the 1955 advertising guidelines. It became clear to the commission that a positive health warning was needed; otherwise any health message could be overcome by the subtleties of modern advertising. To adopt new policy requiring a warning would necessitate overcoming not only the tobacco interests in and out of Congress but also the bureaucratic agencies where resistance could be expected.[18]

Other parts of the bureaucracy were resisting those who were trying to promote a health warning. One of those resisting was, surprisingly enough, the large Department of Health, Education and Welfare (HEW), the parent organization for the Food and Drug Administration (FDA) and the Public Health Service (PHS). Just as siblings frequently are quite different from each other and from their parents, the agencies of health, education and welfare have held remarkably divergent views. From the top, former Secretary Anthony Celebrezze indicated that he thought the government should play no significant role in advising the public of the sup-

[17] A study done by the Bureau of the Census for the Public Health Service in 1956 highlighted the trend toward higher consumption in lower age groups. See: Haenszell, Shimkin, and Millers, *Tobacco Smoking Patterns in the U.S.*, Public Health Monograph No. 45 (1956).

[18] The impact of television advertising on smokers and potential smokers was pointed out in a Federal Trade Commission survey released in 1967. The commission noted the sponsorship of television programs during one week in January of that year. Eighty-seven programs were sponsored in whole or in part by six major cigarette manufacturers. Nearly 1.5 billion viewers watched these programs. (A person who watched ten of the 60 programs was counted as ten viewers.) Approximately 322.7 million were under the age of 21.

posed hazards of cigarette smoking. In mid-1964, Celebrezze wrote
to the chairman of the House Interstate and Foreign Commerce
Committee that the department advised rejection of all those cigarette control bills then pending. He argued that the bills might be
helpful in developing legislation that the department would submit,
but they were, for reasons not explained, unacceptable to the department. HEW never submitted any legislation on cigarettes
and health. Senator Neuberger, referring to the actions of that department, said, "It's fair to infer that they don't want anything [any
labeling requirements] at all." [19] The hesitancy displayed in the
secretary's office was not an accurate index of the feelings on the
smoking and health issue in other parts of the department. The
Public Health Service had undertaken some research in 1957 and
from that time showed some desire to act. When the PHS was
prodded to move by the president in 1964, the agency's quick response was an indication of the extent to which its leadership was
anxious to take some action. After the head of the PHS, Surgeon
General Luther L. Terry, had publicly adopted a position that
favored a health warning, he was sent to Congress to testify on
the labeling requirement bill. He was obliged to state the position
of the secretary of HEW and consequently made it appear that the
PHS did not strongly favor the bill. This unnecessary opposition
helped to split the bureaucracy at a crucial time; it also helped to
insure that meaningful antismoking action would either not be
taken or at least be substantially delayed.

The Food and Drug Administration, the agency that the Surgeon General suggested as the proper regulator of warning requirements, had demonstrated even less interest in the smoking and
health issue than its sister agency, the PHS. The FDA's reluctance
is due, according to Senator Neuberger's book, *Smoke Screen: Tobacco and the Public Welfare*, to a late Victorian episode in congressional politics. She claims that the item "tobacco" appeared in
the 1890 edition of the *U.S. Pharmacopoeia*, an official listing of

[19] Dan Cordtz, "Congress Likely to Vote a Mild Law Requiring Warnings on
Packages," *Wall Street Journal*, March 22, 1965, p. 1.

drugs published by the government. It did not appear in the 1905 or later editions, according to the senator, because the removal of tobacco from the *Pharmacopoeia* was the price that had to be paid to get the support of tobacco state legislators for the Food and Drug Act of 1906. The elimination of the word tobacco automatically removed the leaf from FDA supervision.

The FDA was given what appeared to be another opportunity to concern itself with cigarette smoking when the Hazardous Substances Labeling Act was passed in 1960. It empowered the FDA to control the sale of substances which, among other things, had the capacity to produce illness to man through inhalation. Secretary Celebrezze suggested in a letter to the Senate that the act could be interpreted to cover cigarettes as "hazardous substances." In what had become characteristic behavior of HEW, however, the secretary went on to argue that it would be better to wait and let Congress amend the act to make it more explicit and thereby avoid controversy.[20] Subsequently, Congress rejected such an amendment.

The reluctance of the FDA could be traced to still other factors. During the early 1960s, the agency was having serious problems of its own. It suffered through some devastating investigations conducted by the late Senator Estes Kefauver (D.–Tennessee). The hearings dealt with the pricing practices, safety, and monopoly aspects of the drug industry. One of the alarming revelations to emerge from the hearings was the extent to which the FDA was dominated and supported by that sector of the business community it was supposed to regulate, *i.e.,* drug manufacturers and distributors.[21] In what might have been simple reflex action, the FDA found it easier to keep quiet and follow Secretary Celebrezze's lead to continue to protect its good standing in the business community. The FDA found it expedient to ignore the cigarette health issue even though scientific indictments mounted in the early 1960s and other agencies began to take some action.

[20] *Cigarette Labeling and Advertising* (hearings), 89th Congress, 1st Session, *op. cit.,* p. 22.
[21] For an excellent analysis of the Kefauver drug hearings see: Richard Harris, *The Real Voice* (New York: The Macmillan Company, 1964).

The disparity of views and even the bickering between agencies was allowed to exist up to and through the congressional hearings in 1965. President Johnson made no attempt to coordinate agency programs although he had the administrative mechanism to do so. One of the functions of the Bureau of the Budget (now called the Office of Management and Budget) was to make certain that all agency programs coincided with the president's program. All agency letters sent to Congress, whether favoring or opposing the health warning idea, had to have been cleared by the bureau. The final paragraph of each letter contained these words (or a slight variation of them): "The Bureau of the Budget has advised us it has no objection to the submission of this report from the standpoint of the administration's program."

With the White House publicly silent, the bureaucracy divided among itself, and Congress in the grips of inaction, there appeared to be very little hope for the requirement of a health warning. The tobacco subsystem had been successful in containing the controversy.

At this early stage, the policymaking process resembles a large warehouse of ideas and proposals, with agencies and Congress represented by separate cubicles of various size and importance. Events and participants in the political system might be successful in shifting proposals from one storage cubicle to another, but seldom does this movement result in taking a proposal from the warehouse to a position in the decision-making process where it might be favorably acted upon. Lacking the power to move a proposal results, frequently, in the warehouse becoming a graveyard. The antismoking forces had to find some way to rescue the health warning from the certain oblivion of the political warehouse, where it was already beginning to show signs of atrophy and approaching death.

3

THE ADVISORY COMMITTEE
AND NEW POLICY DIRECTIONS

Moving an issue from obscurity to the top of the government's agenda is a difficult task; there are no guidebooks or manuals detailing the steps in this process. Those who want to initiate change in policy have come to recognize that their cause will succeed only with hard work, careful strategy, and large portions of luck. In consumer affairs, the obstacles to change are nearly overwhelming; they range from the powerful inertia of tradition to forceful opposition from important individuals and groups who see some challenge to their fortunes in whatever policy change is contemplated. Those who oppose government action to protect consumers are better organized and better financed than consumer groups. Lacking the necessary political resources—organization and money—consumer supporters are forced to put together large coalitions of marginal interest groups and work diligently to capture public support.

The decade of the '60s has been called the Decade of the Consumer by some because of the amount of consumer legislation passed by Congress.[1] Although more legislation has been passed than in other periods, its usefulness is somewhat questionable. Cigarette legislation passed in 1965 was of dubious value to the public; it contained a mild health warning requirement for packages but prohibited government agencies from imposing other health rules on cigarette advertising or labeling. The content of the legislation was not the whole story. Once the characteristics of the policy subsystem began to change, the possibilities increased for significant alteration in the policies for which that subsystem had been exclusively responsible.

The public health interests followed a pattern that has been used recently with considerable success by consumer advocates. They located an agency willing to take an action that was unpopular with powerful economic interests and powerfully placed members of Congress. Once the agency acted, the economic interests were forced to react. The reaction brought other agencies, interest groups, and members of Congress into the policy arena. The substance of the initial bureaucratic and congressional actions of the mid-1960s was not as important as the fact that action was taken. The fact that the action compelled future policy to be made in an arena broader than the subsystem that normally controlled smoking and health politics was also significant.

Public support might have been favorable toward the health groups, but it was not well organized or forcefully articulated. Surveys taken by the government in 1964 and 1966 showed between 70 and 75 percent of the public agreeing with the statement, "Cigarette smoking is enough of a health hazard for something to be done

---

[1] In *The Dark Side of the Market Place: The Plight of the American Consumer* (Englewood Cliffs, New Jersey: Prentice-Hall, 1968), Senator Warren Magnuson and Jean Carper discuss what has been done recently for the consumer and what they see as a long and difficult road to more effective protection.

about it." [2] A newspaper poll in 1967, two years after the passage of the first cigarette act, revealed that congressmen favored, two-to-one, a stronger health warning on packages and a requirement that that warning appear in all advertising. More than majority support is sometimes necessary to overcome the power of strongly entrenched interests, however. One of the congressmen surveyed commented, "Let's face it. . . . When you combine the money and power of the tobacco and liquor interests with advertising agencies, newspapers, radio, and television . . . there is too much political muscle involved to expect much accomplishment." [3]

Gaining mass support to overcome the resistance built into policy subsystems is difficult. At certain times in consumer history, a dramatic event or the work of a single individual has provided the impetus necessary to stimulate a change in policy. Upton Sinclair's book, *The Jungle,* on the stenches of the meat packing industry at the turn of the century, and Ralph Nader's forceful volume, *Unsafe at Any Speed,* accusing the automobile industry of irresponsibility in the safety field, are examples of this. The Kefauver drug control legislation was floundering until Frances Kelsey, M.D., shook the conscience of the government with data demonstrating that a sleep-inducing drug called thalidomide, when taken by pregnant women, caused severe, ghastly deformities in babies. Air travel safety systems were expanded and improved after two commercial airplanes collided over the Grand Canyon killing 128 persons. Although the smoking issue was to have its highly visible public advocate, John F. Banzhaf and his group called ASH (Action on Smoking and Health), Banzhaf did not appear until after the first major breakthrough for the health interests. The cigarette issue came to the government's agenda without the backing of organized public opinion.

[2] U.S. Department of Health, Education and Welfare, Public Health Service, National Clearinghouse for Smoking and Health, *Use of Tobacco* (available at the National Clearinghouse, Rockville, Maryland), July, 1969, pp. 431–432.

[3] *Christian Science Monitor,* October 20, 1967.

SUPPORT FOR A HEALTH WARNING

The events that led to action on the smoking and health issue were not as dramatic as the events that led to action on other consumer issues. They were characteristic, however, of the manner in which bureaucrats and members of Congress draw on each other's assets to bring an issue into public view. Developing support for a health warning was not easy, but the success of the supporters of the warning is an indication of the political power latent within the bureaucracy. When this power is skillfully marshalled, change can be initiated.

Three related occurrences set the policymaking process in motion. The first of these was a Senate Joint Resolution (SJR 174) introduced by Senator Neuberger in March 1962, which called for the establishment of a presidential commission on tobacco and health. Congressional action was predictable; Congress was not interested in the resolution. There were no hearings, little discussion, and SJR 174 seemed to face certain death. Senator Neuberger knew from experience that Congress would do little on the smoking issue because of the support the tobacco industry had. Furthermore, if the resolution had passed, it would have only encouraged, not required, the president to establish a study commission. This suggests that the senator was seeking a wider audience than Congress. Her resolution provided the health interests with an opportunity to rally and take the idea to the president or directly to the public, knowing that Congress was unlikely to respond. It first appeared that the resolution was not the appropriate vehicle. Senator Neuberger's resolution lay dormant for two months. Had it not been for the efforts of an enterprising reporter, it might have been interred forever in the legislative graveyard.

Spurred by the suggestion in the resolution of a presidential commission, a reporter at one of President Kennedy's major news conferences asked the president what he intended to do about the question of smoking and health. These live televised news conferences put the president under considerable pressure to appear calm, knowledgeable, and confident. President Kennedy had earned the reputation of handling questions at these conferences with skill and poise. Adept in answering questions, witty, and most important, thoroughly briefed by his staff on what questions the press might be expected to raise, he was seldom embarrassed.

Lengthy briefing sessions preceded each press conference, but the briefing for the conference in May 1962 must not have included the smoking and health issue. When the president was asked whether he or his advisors agreed with the findings of an increasing number of studies that linked smoking and ill health, there was an embarrassing pause. Then the response came awkwardly:

> The—that matter is sensitive enough and the stock market is in sufficient difficulty without my giving you an answer which is not based on complete information, which I don't have, and therefore perhaps we could—I'd be glad to respond to that question in more detail next week. . . .[4]

As a result of the press conference, the issue was moved from Congress to the president. He was now publicly committed to initiating some action within the bureaucracy. The pressure of public opinion, combined with pressure from those bureaucrats who saw an opening they had been waiting for, guaranteed a speedy presidential response. Soon after the press conference, President Kennedy asked the Public Health Service to report on what it had been doing in the field of smoking and health. The agency had done a considerable amount, although its activities were not well known. Officials of the PHS were aware of the smoking studies done by medical scientists and had even done some of their own. In 1957, the PHS had published the report of a study group that assessed the smoking and health data available at that time. The report concluded that excessive smoking was one of the causal factors in lung cancer. Soon after its release, the report was officially endorsed by the PHS.

4 The *New York Times,* May 24, 1962, p. 16.

The Public Health Service is a favored agency of Congress. It seldom has trouble obtaining its appropriation, and sometimes it receives more than it requests for specialized health research. However, when it attempts to sell programs like air pollution control or occupational safety, it encounters considerable resistance. When the White House expressed interest in the research of the Public Health Service in terms that indicated that the research findings might be implemented, the PHS responded enthusiastically. Only two weeks after the press conference, Surgeon General Luther Terry announced he would establish a high-level advisory committee to study the impact of smoking on health. The appointment of the committee was the culmination of the events that gave the health warning issue the momentum it needed to eventually receive serious consideration as national policy.

ADVISORY COMMITTEES
IN THE BUREAUCRACY

This committee was not the same kind of organization as the presidential commission envisioned by Senator Neuberger. Advisory committees have been used by the bureaucracy for a long time. They are designed to bring outside views into bureaucratic policymaking, usually at the stage where new policies are being considered. Some advisory committees are made up entirely of experts who provide an agency with the special kinds of information it could not expect to get from its own staff. Others, called representative advisory committees, are composed of those who represent some special interest. Representative committees serve at least two useful functions for the agency they advise: they inject some new, outside ideas that might not otherwise find their way into agency policy, and they serve as sounding boards for testing agency proposals.

Both the representative and the expert advisory committee can be used for political purposes. The Surgeon General's Advisory Committee on Smoking and Health was an expert committee. Its purposes, however, were as much political as scientific. The report of a high-level committee of well-known, respected experts was bound to have a significant impact on the public. The forcefulness of that impact could be heightened if selection of committee members, reports of their meetings, and announcement of their findings were handled with political skill and an appreciation for the nature of public opinion. The Surgeon General must have sensed that the Advisory Committee and its recommendations would give the Public Health Service the support it needed to pursue programs designed to reduce the health threat posed by the mass consumption of cigarettes. The events that followed the announcement that a committee would be created proved that at least some physicians and bureaucrats knew the politics of policymaking very well.

The first clues to the political dimensions of the Surgeon General's committee appeared early. One was that the committee was to make no new scientific study of its own. Instead, its mandate was to assess the value of existing studies and their conclusions. This had already been done on a small scale by private health groups and earlier by the Public Health Service itself. It was important to the Public Health Service to have a new, outside group review the results of the existing studies. The Advisory Committee was well suited to giving the existing studies new currency in the public eye.

Another clue to the political nature of the committee was the manner in which the 12 (later 10) men were selected. The Surgeon General stated publicly that the group was to include scientific, professional persons concerned with all aspects of smoking and health. The tobacco industry, health groups, professional associations, and federal agencies were called upon to participate in selecting individuals who might serve on the committee.[5]

The names of 150 scientists were presented to those groups involved in the selection process. These groups were to eliminate from consideration individuals for any reason they saw fit and return the list to the Surgeon General. One "blackball" apparently could have

[5] Those groups asked to suggest people for the committee were: American Cancer Society; American Medical Association; Tobacco Institute, Inc.; Food and Drug Administration; National Tuberculosis Association; Federal Trade Commission; and the United States Office of Science and Technology.

eliminated any name from consideration for appointment. From the approved lists the Surgeon General selected the members of the Advisory Committee on Smoking and Health.

The selection process underscores the great pains to which the Surgeon General went to make certain that the report of the committee would not be attacked on the grounds that the membership was stacked against any particular interest. To further protect the committee from such an attack, anyone who had made any public statements on the smoking and health controversy was ineligible to serve. The gentleman named to serve as executive director of the committee was removed shortly after he was appointed. Learning of the appointment, reporters from his hometown newspaper asked for a comment. The response they received was that recent studies definitely suggested that tobacco was a health hazard.[6] The neutral integrity of the committee was thus challenged, and a new executive director was appointed.

The men appointed to the Advisory Committee were among the most distinguished members of their professions. Eight of the members were M.D.'s with specialization in fields such as internal medicine, epidemiology, and pharmacology. The nonphysicians were a chemist and a statistician. All of the men were professors at leading medical schools with the exception of Dr. Eugene H. Guthrie, the panel's staff director, who was a veteran of 12 years with the Public Health Service. There were three cigarette smokers in the group and two who smoked pipes and cigars on occasion.[7]

With the increasing participation of the bureaucracy in policy-making, advisory committees (or councils, as they are sometimes

[6] Maurine B. Neuberger, *Smoke Screen: Tobacco and the Public Welfare* (Englewood Cliffs, New Jersey: Prentice-Hall, 1963).

[7] Members of the Advisory Committee were: Dr. Eugene H. Guthrie, Public Health Service, the committee's staff director; Dr. Stanhope Bayne-Jones, Walter Reed Army Institute of Research; Dr. Walter J. Burdette, University of Utah; William G. Cochran, Harvard University; Dr. Emmanuel Farber, University of Pittsburgh; Dr. Louis F. Fieser, Harvard University; Dr. Jacob Furth, Columbia University; Dr. John B. Hickman, Indiana University; Dr. Charles A. LeMaistre, University of Texas; Dr. Leonard M. Schuman, University of Minnesota; and Dr. Maurice H. Seevers, University of Michigan.

called) seem to offer a way of keeping bureaucrats in tune with public opinion. Every agency now has at least one, usually several, of these councils. In 1972 there were more than 1,400 federal advisory committees reporting to over 50 agencies of the federal government. There were 367 committees in HEW alone.

The popularity of advisory committees waned as it became more apparent that representation within the bureaucratic decision-making process had its drawbacks as well as its virtues. Due to the specialized activities of agencies, membership on advisory committees tends to be specialized. These specialized interests often reinforce the biases and positions taken by the agency, making it even more difficult for outsiders representing a nonspecialized, broader interest to have any influence on policymaking. The symbiotic relationship between agencies and those it might have an obligation to regulate makes many observers skeptical of the value of advisory committees as vehicles for public interest representation.[8]

The quality and usefulness of advisory committees has always varied greatly. The Surgeon General's group was highly regarded because of the impressive academic and scientific credentials of its members. Other committees are much less impressive. One observer has been unkind enough to suggest that committee memberships have become attractive and meaningless patronage jobs in a society where the number of high-level patronage positions is not increasing as fast as the population. Usually members are unpaid; the rewards for membership are mostly political and psychological. A presidential certificate of appointment to an advisory commission or one signed by a cabinet officer is an impressive trophy. There might even be an opportunity to pose for a photograph with a high-level official. This, in addition to the satisfaction of serving, is adequate com-

8 Avery Leiserson, in *Administrative Regulation: A Study in Representation of Interests* (Chicago: University of Chicago Press, 1942), discusses the history and early use of advisory councils in bureaucracies. More recent discussions of advisory committees can be found in William W. Boyer, *Bureaucracy on Trial: Policy Making by Government Agencies* (Indianapolis: The Bobbs-Merrill Company, 1964) and Thomas E. Cronin and Norman C. Thomas, "Educational Policy Advisors and the Great Society," *Public Policy*, Vol. XVIII, No. 5, Fall, 1970.

pensation for some.[9] The old Business Advisory Council, discussed later in this chapter, was a powerful and direct link between government and business. The rewards for service on it included the opportunity to insure the right of self-regulation for the business community. The Surgeon General's committee, unlike others, was not established to reward the politically loyal or provide industry with the chance to escape government controls.

The names of those selected for the committee were announced on October 27, 1962. Shortly thereafter, the members, who were paid consultant's fees, began their work. Other consultants were also hired, and six professional staff members of the Public Health Service were assigned to the committee.

THE SURGEON GENERAL'S COMMITTEE AT WORK

The newly formed Advisory Committee on Smoking and Health met for the first time on November 9, 1962. At this meeting the committee agreed on its operating procedures. They agreed to first review the scientific literature on all aspects of the use of tobacco and smoking habits. Other possible contributing factors to ill health such as air pollution, industrial exposure, radiation, and alcohol were also included in the committee's agenda.

The full committee held nine meetings of two to four days' duration during 1963, and there were several meetings of subcommittees. The witnesses who appeared were consultants hired by the committee and representatives of special interest groups, including the tobacco industry. A transcript was kept but not made public. In fact, a great degree of secrecy surrounded all activities of the Advisory Committee. The extraordinary precautions taken to assure there would be no leaks were so out of character for the Public Health Service that tensions were exaggerated for those who already

[9] The use of advisory committee positions as patronage is discussed by Don Oberdorfer in "The New Political Non-Job," *Harper's Magazine,* October, 1965.

entertained substantial fears about the content of the committee's report. It probably was necessary for the PHS to take precautions to prevent erroneous information from spreading through rumors. The secrecy did serve another function, however. It provided some suspense, and by the time the report was ready to be released, all the major news agencies of the nation focused their attention on the Advisory Committee.

In Washington, even the most tightly sealed conferences emit some information to the press. There was substantial speculation about the committee's meetings taking place deep within the confines of Public Health Service headquarters in Washington's elegant suburb, Bethesda, Maryland. Virtually none of the speculation gave any comfort to those whose fortunes were dependent upon the sale of tobacco and tobacco products.

THE ADVISORY COMMITTEE'S REPORT

On Saturday, January 11, 1964, the world discovered what had made the tobacco interests uneasy. In a well-prepared, carefully staged news conference, the Surgeon General announced the results of the Advisory Committee's study.[10] The conference was held behind locked doors in the State Department auditorium, the same room used by President Kennedy for his meetings with the press. With the reporters seated and the television newsreel cameras in place, the Surgeon General and his committee took seats on the stage. The large "no smoking" signs affixed to the walls on both sides of the raised platform were unintentional indices of the tone of the conference that was to follow. The reporters were given 90 minutes to ask questions and read the published 387-page committee report. At the end of 90 minutes the doors were opened, the re-

10 U.S. Department of Health, Education and Welfare, *Smoking and Health: Report of the Advisory Committee to the Surgeon General of the Public Health Service,* Public Health Service Document No. 1103 (Washington, D.C.: U.S. Government Printing Office, 1964).

porters released, and the results of the study were telegraphed around the country and the world.

The selection of a Saturday for the day of the press conference had some significance. It signaled that the report might adversely affect the price of tobacco shares on the nation's stock exchanges. When the smoking and health issue was first raised in 1954, there were pronounced adverse effects on tobacco shares. Further revelations did not seem to affect the market, for almost without pause cigarette sales increased.[11] Tobacco shares were not experiencing the same lively recovery that the stock markets as a whole enjoyed after 1962, but adverse health reports were being taken in stride by the time the Advisory Committee's report was issued.[12]

The bold-face summaries of the committee's work were forceful enough for reasonable men to anticipate an unfavorable reaction in the stock market and in certain other quarters. These summaries read, "Cigarette smoking is causally related to lung cancer in men; the magnitude of the effect of cigarette smoking far outweighs all other factors. The data for women, though less extensive, point in the same direction." [13] The report included detailed summaries of the studies that the committee had considered. These studies established a positive relationship between cigarette smoking and a host of other diseases. But the report indicated that although smoking was related to higher death rates from such things as cardiovascular diseases and cirrhosis of the liver, a causal relationship had not been definitely established in these ailments. There was scant encouragement in the report for those who smoked cigars and pipes. Although the evidence of the ill effects from these tobacco products was not

[11] Cigarette sales were 14 percent less the month after the report was issued than they had been in that month of the preceding year. The drop was temporary, however; sales recovered and were off imperceptibly for that year.

[12] The first trading day after the press conference, some prices fell slightly, but one, Reynolds Tobacco, closed higher. Cigar shares profited from their more favorable treatment by the committee. Some of these gained more than $2 a share.

[13] *Smoking and Health: Report of the Advisory Committee to the Surgeon General of the Public Health Service,* Public Health Service Publication No. 1103, 1964, p. 37.

as devastating as for cigarettes, there was indication that their consumption was related to high mortality ratios for ". . . cancers of
the mouth, esophagus, larynx and lung, and for stomach and duo-
denal ulcers."

At the press conference, the Surgeon General noted that the
precise role of smoking in causing chronic diseases was not established by the studies. The Advisory Committee agreed, however,
that it was more prudent from the public health viewpoint to accept
the cause-and-effect relationship that the data indicated than to wait
until the exact relationship had been determined. In short, the
members of the committee concluded unanimously that "Cigarette
smoking is a health hazard of sufficient importance in the United
States to warrant appropriate remedial action."

Occasionally, advisory committees have become significant
forces in agency policymaking; at times they have come to control
the agency and its work. The Advisory Committee on Smoking and
Health was a significant force in the policy process, but it was not a
lasting one. The committee had a life span of little more than a
year. By contrast, the Business Advisory Council (BAC) of the Department of Commerce was an important force in United States
commercial policymaking for neary 30 years.[14]

The Business Advisory Council was privy to decision making in
the Department of Commerce and other agencies because it boasted
an extremely prestigious and powerful membership. Corporate leaders, who made up the 60-man council, had close ties with the White
House, particularly during the Eisenhower years. The group met in
secrecy about six times each year. Cabinet members tripped over
each other for invitations to speak before the council at such swank
resorts as Hot Springs, Virginia, and Pebble Beach, California.

No one really knows just how powerful the Business Advisory
Council was, but many outsiders suspected that it wielded more
power than it should have. A committee of the House of Representatives decided to investigate the BAC in 1955, but the council

[14] Robert J. Donovan, *Eisenhower: The Inside Story* (New York: Harper
Brothers, 1956), p. 341.

denied the committee access to its files. The committee reprimanded agencies for allowing groups like the BAC to make their decisions for them. For example, the committee said that one bureau within the Department of Commerce

> has effected a virtual abdication of administrative responsibility on the part of Government officials in charge of the Department of Commerce in that their actions in many instances are but the automatic approval of decisions already made outside the Government in business and industry.[15]

CONTROLLING ADVISORY COMMITTEES

As early as the 1940s, the government had tried to eliminate, or at least limit, the excesses of some advisory committees. The Justice Department issued regulations governing agendas and the selection of committee chairmen. All of these regulations were written so that agencies would have more complete control of their committees. Congressional concern appeared in the middle 1950s with the hearings mentioned above and some activity of the House Committee on Government Operations.

In 1962 President Kennedy issued an executive order establishing regulations concerning the use of advisory committees by the federal government. President Nixon issued an executive order in June 1972 that established a centralized management system for controlling advisory groups. After hearings on advisory committee management by the House Government Operations Subcommittee on Legal and Monetary Affairs and the Senate Government Operations Subcommittee on Intergovernmental Relations, the Congress passed the Federal Advisory Committee Act (P.L. 92-463), which the presi-

---

[15] *Interim Report of the Antitrust Subcommittee of the Committee on the Judiciary on WOC's and Government Advisory Groups,* U.S. House of Representatives, 84th Congress, 2nd Session (1956), p. 99. An excellent analysis of business influence in government, including a discussion of the use and abuse of advisory councils, can be found in: Grant McConnell, *Private Power and American Democracy* (New York: Alfred A. Knopf, 1966), pp. 276–279.

dent signed on October 6, 1972. The law is under the supervision of the Committee Management Secretariat in the Office of Management and Budget (OMB), and has been implemented by OMB Circular A-63.

In the first annual Federal Advisory Committee Report by the president to Congress in March 1973, it was noted, "In the current calendar year (1974) we expect to reduce advisory committees to the minimum essential number." [16] The law provides that the function of all committees should be strictly advisory and that any committee whose duration is not fixed by law must terminate its activities no more than two years after it is established.[17] Nevertheless, the power of advisory groups still depends on the degree of enthusiasm bureaucrats have for following their advice. Where the departmental ethos is one of close cooperation with the groups that that department regulates, abuses will continue. Advisory committees will succeed in representing broad spectrums of the public only when agencies make a determined effort to include within their structure individuals with divergent and even conflicting points of view.

The selection techniques employed by the Surgeon General and the reputation of the Advisory Committee's members assured that there would be little criticism of the committee itself. The Surgeon General held his committee in very high esteem and he worked closely with it. He officially accepted the committee's report within 16 days of its completion, although the Department of Health, Education and Welfare, itself, was less than enthusiastic about the report and its political implications. Immediately after its acceptance, Dr. Terry moved to clean his own house of those products the report had indicted. He ordered a halt to the free distribution of cigarettes in the 16 public hospitals and 50 Indian hospitals under the direc-

16 U.S. Office of Management and Budget, Federal Advisory Committees: First Annual Report of the President (Washington, D.C.: Government Printing Office, March 1973).

17 All meetings have to be called by a government employee; the agency retains the right to draft the agenda; and all meetings are open to the public. Also, the meetings are conducted by an agency employee who is empowered to adjourn the meeting whenever he determines that adjournment would be in the public interest.

tion of the Public Health Service; the staff members of those hospitals were ordered to conduct educational programs to discourage cigarette smoking.

A measure of the political success that the Advisory Committee on Smoking and Health experienced was the speed with which other agencies rallied to the antismoking cause. One week after the Advisory Committee's report was issued, the Federal Trade Commission announced that it would issue rules governing the advertising and labeling of cigarettes. The announcement was accompanied by a draft of the proposed rules and an invitation for all interested parties to submit their views to the commission.[18]

The impact of the Surgeon General's report on the political system was just what the antismoking interests had hoped for. It provided the Federal Trade Commission with an opportunity to make its move. Shortly after the commission made its plans known to the public, the House Committee on Interstate and Foreign Commerce and the Senate Committee on Commerce announced they would hold hearings on cigarettes, their consumption, and their effect on public health. The Advisory Committee, by bringing the issue into focus, gave the subsystem a blow that has probably proved fatal. The bureaucracy was given the backing it needed to spring into action. But before the bureaucracy could succeed in implementing its policy, congressional resistance had to be overcome. Congress was to make it clear that it still had a great deal to say about what policy would be made and how it would be made. Congress was soon to rescue the cigarette manufacturers, at least temporarily, from the potentially damaging proposals of the Federal Trade Commission and the Public Health Service.

[18] The notice was published in the *Federal Register* on January 22, 1964, four days after the Federal Trade Commission made the announcement, 29 *Federal Register*, pp. 530–532 (1964).

4

DEVELOPMENT OF
ADMINISTRATIVE
POLICYMAKING POWERS

The Federal Trade Commission's announcement of its intention to require a health warning was a reminder to everyone that agencies have the power to make policy. The cigarette interests were not pleased by the announcement, although they had every reason to expect it. They knew that Trade Commission policymaking would be different in both procedure and outcome from congressional policymaking, because agency personnel were much less sympathetic to the tobacco position than were congressmen. Lobbyists make it their business to know where they are likely to receive the most favorable decisions, and those representing business and industry have come to view Congress as being more responsive to them than the bureaucracy.

The strategy of the tobacco men was to question Federal Trade Commission authority to make policy involving a cigarette health warning and thereby insure that the final policy decision would be made by Congress, not the FTC. Consequently, in their argument against the commission's announcement of its intention to require a health warning, the tobacco interests raised with skill and eloquence some of the most basic questions that have stalked the growth of agency policymaking powers. For example, they asked how, in a democratic form of government, nonelected bureaucrats could be permitted to exercise powers of government that are constitutionally allocated to elected representatives of the people. How could so important a matter, one affecting a large industry and thousands, perhaps millions, of people, be decided by bureaucrats? How were those associated with the tobacco interests to participate in the policy process when the policymakers were not subject to popular control through elections? And, how might they hold the administrative decision makers responsible for their decisions when they had no electoral process to resort to? These questions were then and are now fundamentally important to any system of representative government.

CONGRESSIONAL DELEGATION OF AUTHORITY

The basis of the complaints of the cigarette interests rested in the clear language of Article I of the Constitution—"All legislative powers herein granted shall be vested in a Congress of the United States. . . ." There is nothing in other sections of the document to indicate that legislative or policymaking powers should reside in the bureaucracy. Yet the accumulation of policy powers in the legislature has never worked well, and from the beginning Congress has been obliged to find ways to share its powers.

Although legislative bodies theoretically could write and enact all the rules that govern society, it is seldom practical for them to do so. For a time, Congress and state legislatures tried it. They grappled with many complex policy issues that experience has now taught them to entrust to administrative agencies. Railroad rates and other matters of a regulatory nature, for example, were once written by legislatures. Yet, almost from the time the Constitution was adopted, Congress recognized that it could not effectively handle all of the complexities of policymaking. There are natural limitations on legislatures that make them incapable of acting as effective policymakers under certain conditions.

These conditions arise when policy decisions involving complex and technical knowledge are called for. Congress does not have sufficient expertise or the necessary time to devote to the details of much modern policymaking. There is no good way to write legislation that is sufficiently clairvoyant to foresee all of the individual cases and circumstances that are bound to arise in the administration of policy in a dynamic, complex society. Under these conditions, policy has to be made incrementally, over extended periods of time. Career experts in the bureaucracy are in a better position to devote continued attention to a particular problem and develop policy standards and guidelines than are members of Congress. If Congress were to enact all the specific rules and regulations necessary for the administration of programs, one of two equally undesirable results would occur: the rules would be too general to serve as effective guidelines for administrators, or they would be too rigid and inflexible and so would become useless in short order. In delegating policymaking powers to agencies, Congress relieves itself of the burden of detailed work and frees itself to devote time to issues of basic policy.

Under delegated authority, agencies shape, mold, and even change policies set down by Congress in legislation. When Congress authorizes the creation of an agency or a new program, there is usually little reference to the details of implementing the program. Instead of writing an operations manual that would guide the agency through all situations, Congress usually states simply that a program should be carried out in a "just" or "reasonable" manner. A phrase that sometimes appears in legislation is the mandate that an agency perform "in the public interest, convenience and necessity." The vagueness of such instructions or guidelines allows an agency considerable latitude in making policy as it sees fit.

The official policymaking process might be thought of as taking place in three consecutive stages. The first is legislative, involving Congress and the president, i.e., congressional passage and presidential approval of a bill. The remaining two stages are administrative. The second has been alluded to by the late Supreme Court Justice Robert Jackson: "It may clarify the proper administrative function . . . to think of [congressional] legislation as unfinished law which the administrative body must complete before it is ready for application." [1] In this stage the agencies clarify legislation by writing detailed regulations or rules. The third stage occurs when a program is being administered. At that point, policy is made and altered to account for changing conditions. There is a possible fourth stage—review by Congress or the courts. Congress, through its oversight procedures, can change the handiwork of an agency as it changed the Federal Trade Commission policy in the cigarette controversy. By writing new legislation, changing appropriations, or simply threatening to do these things, Congress can make its influence felt. And whether or not Congress acts, judicial review of agency policymaking might reverse or substantially alter what an agency has done.

As the problems of society become more complex, Congress tends to rely increasingly on agencies for policymaking. American society has already reached a point where administrative agencies are producing more policy than the other two branches of the government combined. Agencies are performing functions that could be assigned to either the courts or the legislature. One observer, former Commissioner Lee Loevinger of the Federal Communications Commission, has compared the frequency of agency policymaking with that of Congress and the courts:

> While the courts handle thousands of cases each year and Congress produces hundreds of laws each year, the administrative agencies

[1] *Federal Trade Commission v. Ruberoid*, 343 US 470 (1952).

handle hundreds of thousands of matters annually. The administrative agencies are engaged in the mass production of law, in contrast to the courts, which are engaged in the handicraft production of law.[2]

One cannot quantify and measure amounts of policymaking with precision. Yet it is not unreasonable to conclude that in terms of policy decisions that directly affect persons and property, administrative agencies are today of major importance.[3]

Production of law by agencies could be dangerous for representative government. If there were no way for elected officials or an independent judiciary to control administrative decisions, policymaking by an independent bureaucracy would negate traditional theories of representation upon which democratic systems are built. As indicated earlier, such traditional theories imply that means are available for citizens to both participate in policymaking and hold government accountable for the decisions it makes.[4] The effectiveness of democratic controls on agency policymaking has been questioned for many years, as the history of the Federal Trade Commission and other agencies shows. The protestations of the tobacco

[2] Lee Loevinger, "The Administrative Agency as a Paradigm of Government —A Survey of the Administrative Process," *Indiana Law Journal*, Vol. 40, No. 3 (Spring 1965), p. 305. Justice Jackson noted the rise of administrative powers in a now famous dissent, "The rise of administrative bodies probably has been the most significant legal trend of the last century and perhaps more values today are affected by their decisions than by those of all the courts. . . . They also have begun to have important consequences on personal rights. They have become a veritable fourth branch of Government, which has deranged our three branch legal theories much as the concept of a fourth dimension unsettles our three-dimensional thinking." *Federal Trade Commission v. Ruberoid*, 343 US 470 (1952).

[3] The Administrative Conference of the United States claims there are more than 30 departments and agencies that have power to make decisions affecting individual rights. Congress created the conference in 1964, but the president failed to appoint a chairman until 1968. It has as its members most of the agencies of the government. Each year the conference develops recommendations to Congress and the president for improvements in agency procedures that affect the rights of private persons and business interests through administratvie investigation, adjudication, licensing, rulemaking, ratemaking, claims determination, and other proceedings.

[4] See pp. 13–14.

lobbyists were a modern revival of all the most difficult questions about agency policymaking that had been raised in the past. Yet, the actions of the FTC in the cigarette labeling controversy show that in some circumstances bureaucratic policymaking can enhance the representational qualities of government.

Although there are serious theoretical and practical obstacles to the delegation of policymaking authority agencies have been operating under the umbrella of delegated authority for many years. In only two cases has the Supreme Court held congressional delegations to be unconstitutional.[5] Consequently, many claim there is little question about the ability and legality of Congress to delegate. The law on this point seems so firm to one authority on administrative law that he has commented, "Lawyers who try to win cases by arguing that congressional delegations are unconstitutional almost invariably do more harm than good to their clients' interests." [6] Nevertheless, this constitutional issue, as any other, is within the discretion of the Court. Consequently, the question of limits on delegation can never be defined for all times with precision. The tobacco interests' strategy against the commission's action was based in part on the claim that Congress had stopped short of providing authority to the FTC to issue so-called trade regulation rules. The position of the Tobacco Institute in regard to the FTC is summarized in the following words:

> . . . in terms of policy and discretion, whatever substantive regulation may be believed to be necessary in this area of smoking and health, Congress alone should enact it.
> . . . we respectfully submit that in these proposed Trade Regulation Rules the Commission is not exercising the authority conferred upon it by Congress in the Federal Trade Commission Act. It is plainly legislating.[7]

5 *Panama Refining Company v. Ryan,* 293 US 388 (1935) and *Schechter Poultry Corporation v. United States,* 295 US 495 (1935).

6 Kenneth Culp Davis, *Administrative Law and Government* (St. Paul: West Publishing Company, 1960), p. 55.

7 From the statement on behalf of the Tobacco Institute, Inc., submitted to the Federal Trade Commission, p. 6 (mimeo.).

The tobacco interests must have recognized that their argument was, at the very least, risky, in view of what the Supreme Court had been saying for years about delegation. Their approach was nonetheless astute in more than one respect. Important segments of public opinion could be expected to rally to the cry that faceless administrators were performing a role that should be reserved to the elected representatives of the people. The powerful industrial and commercial communities could be expected to be sympathetic with that view. Furthermore, by arguing the delegation issue, they were able to gain the attention of Congress and thus increase the possibility that the controversy would be transferred, eventually, from the commission to Congress.

On April 4, 1972, one industrial group, the National Petroleum Refiners Association achieved a ruling in the U.S. District Court which declared that the FTC lacked the statutory authority to issue trade regulation rules. The immediate issue concerned whether or not the commission could issue a rule requiring octane ratings on gasoline pumps. The U.S. Court of Appeals reversed the District Court on June 27, 1973, and upheld the commission's authority to make binding rules.

Questioning the power of Congress to delegate and the limits of its delegations, challenges the concept of administrative policymaking and, indeed, the nature of a policy process in which powers are shared by several institutions of government. Since the legality of delegation is so important to the administrative system in general, one profits from a closer examination of the causes that have prompted Congress to delegate authority and the basis for judicial approval of such action. The history of the Federal Trade Commission and its early responsibilities in the antitrust field are relevant to the understanding of these subjects.

REGULATORY AUTHORITY DELEGATED
TO FEDERAL TRADE COMMISSION

In the latter part of the 19th century, the nation experienced the growth of large industrial enterprises that cornered large shares of the market for various commodities. The notion that one or a few companies should control a market ran counter to the time-honored, laissez-faire ideal of vigorous competition. State regulation proved to be largely ineffective in breaking up or preventing the creation of large monopolies, partially because many of them were national in scope. The federal government entered the "trust-busting" picture with the passage of the Sherman Act in 1890. The Sherman Act required that the government rely for policy development on vague, legislative language and judicial decisions. The act created no administrative agency; no policymaking authority was delegated by Congress. The statements of major purpose in the first two sections alert the reader to the problems of enforcement that were to develop:

> *Section 1* Every contract, combination in the form of trust . . . or conspiracy in restraint of trade or commerce . . . is hereby declared to be illegal. . . .
>
> *Section 2* Every person who shall monopolize, or combine or conspire with any other person or persons, to monopolize . . . shall be deemed guilty of a misdemeanor. . . .

The language of these sections required further definition. Who was to define what constituted "a conspiracy in restraint of trade," for example? There was no answer to this question in the Sherman Act, although by implication the burden fell on the federal courts.

Thirteen years after passage of the act, the Antitrust Division was established within the Department of Justice to investigate and initiate prosecution of those corporations and individuals who violated the Sherman Act. Almost immediately, the division encountered serious difficulty. The wording of the act provided very few guidelines for prosecution, and the division had to develop workable definitions or guidelines from the act's general language. Without delegated policymaking powers from Congress, the division found its job exceedingly difficult and, eventually, close to impossible.

The only technique available for developing standards was the case-by-case method. Alleged violators of the act had to be taken to court. The judges, on the basis of the information presented, decided whether or not the challenged action violated the Sherman Act. This proved to be an unsatisfactory way of developing standards. It was not only slow, awkward, and unpredictable, but it relied on judges who might or might not have been fully aware of the intricacies of corporate finance and economics. The courts were confronted with a wide range of cases; judges could not afford to specialize in these vastly complicated matters. The results were that no hard or firm standards emerged under the Sherman Act. Nearly all questions that could conceivably arise under the act had to be tested in the courts, but it was difficult to rely on precedent because cases differed sufficiently from one another to make the formulation of rules of general applicability virtually impossible.

Uncertainty grew as a result of reliance on the courts for interpretation. Neither the government nor the corporate giants knew what might violate the Sherman Act. The pinnacle of uncertainty was reached in 1911 with two Supreme Court decisions, one involving the Standard Oil Company, the other the American Tobacco Company.[8] In these cases, the Court wrote what came to be called the "rule of reason." Basically, the Court said that only *unreasonable* restraints of trade or monopolies were in violation of the Sherman Act. These decisions underscored the frustration of the Court in dealing with antitrust policy. Nothing was clarified; in fact, the situation was made even more difficult because there was another term that begged for definition. What constituted an "unreasonable" restraint of trade? Where would the courts draw the line between what was "reasonable" and what was "unreasonable"? [9]

[8] *Standard Oil Company v. United States,* 221 US 1 (1911) and *American Tobacco Company v. United States,* 221 US 106 (1911).
[9] See Gerard C. Henderson, *The FTC: A Study in Administrative Law and*

The experience of the government with the Sherman Act dramatized the need for Congress to delegate policymaking power to an administrative agency. It was clear that reliance on the courts for policymaking would result in an inadequate body of law, unpredictable and difficult to enforce. The antitrust situation grew more and more critical. President Taft expressed the fears of many when he stated that judicial involvement in antitrust policymaking "might involve our whole judicial system in disaster." [10]

Concerned members of Congress realized that the Sherman Act had to be modified. Some members thought that the modification ought to be in the direction of making the act more explicit. They wanted to spell out in detailed legislation the corporate actions that violated the Sherman Act. This delineation would have eliminated or reduced reliance on the courts for the development of enforcement standards, according to those who favored this approach. Others disagreed. They argued that Congress was not well equipped to write the detailed legislation necessary; furthermore, Senator Newlands of Nevada argued that it would be unwise to attempt to write detailed legislation to clarify the Sherman Act. He said on the floor of the Senate, "If there were 20 bad trade practices today and you were to name them in law and condemn them, there would be others established tomorrow." [11] Continuity and expertise were needed to enforce antitrust policy. The Senator supported the creation of an administrative board that would have both enforcement and policymaking powers. The Interstate Commerce Commission, which had been established in 1887, served as Senator Newlands's model. A commission of this sort, he reasoned, could develop precedents, traditions, and a continuous policy based on orderly experience in enforcement and in the refinement of guidelines. The views

---

Procedure (New Haven: Yale University Press, 1924), for a thoughtful discussion of the enforcement problem.

[10] *Congressional Record,* 61st Congress, 2nd Session, p. 382, quoted in Henderson, *op. cit.,* p. 16.

[11] *Congressional Record,* Senate, June 13, 1914, 63rd Congress, 2nd Session, p. 11084.

of Senator Newlands prevailed, and the Federal Trade Commission was established by Congress in 1914.

The same year the Federal Trade Commission was created, Congress passed the Clayton Act. Passage of this act showed that Congress was not yet willing to give up its prerogative of writing detailed regulations for an agency such as the FTC. In an attempt to refine the Sherman Act by legislating regulations, the Clayton Act detailed those actions of corporations or individuals that were prohibited. Thus, for example, the Clayton Act prohibits price discrimination, if the purpose or effect of such discrimination is to lessen competition or create a monopoly. This congressional attempt to be more explicit did not withstand the tests of time and experience. The provisions of the Clayton Act were still too broad and ill defined to provide enlightened guidance for effective enforcement. The courts would have remained the principal policymaker in the antitrust field had Congress not created the Federal Trade Commission, for neither the Clayton Act nor the Sherman Act ended the need for interpretation by the courts. It eventually fell, at least in part, to the Federal Trade Commission to interpret and enforce the provisions of the Clayton Act, thereby reducing some of the burden on the courts.

The process of experimentation with antitrust policymaking at the turn of the century has been repeated in other areas of public policy. Whenever standards have had to be developed for the administration of new and continuing programs, Congress has increasingly found it practical to empower bureaucratic agencies to do the task. Since agencies are better equipped to carry out the task of filling out the skeletal programs that Congress legislates, they have, over the years, received increased policymaking responsibilities. However, when Congress delegates powers to the bureaucracy, questions about the separation of powers are bound to arise.

THE SUPREME COURT ON DELEGATION

From the earliest days of our constitutional history, Congress has found it necessary to delegate certain of its powers to bureaucratic agencies. The Supreme Court held unconstitutional delegations in only the two cases previously cited, both of which were decided in 1935. One suspects that the decisions in these cases were more closely allied to the Court's skepticism of New Deal programs than to genuine concern about violation of the separation of powers doctrine. For years prior to 1935, the Court had upheld delegation after delegation. While doing so, the justices inserted into their opinions statements on the inviolability of the separation thesis. In one of the earliest cases involving this question, the Court wrote a reaffirmation of the separation principle while upholding the delegation itself:

> . . . it is essential to the successful working of this system that the persons entrusted with power in any one of these branches (executive, legislative and judicial) shall not be permitted to encroach upon the powers confided to the others, but that each by the law of its creation be limited to the exercise of the powers appropriate to its own department and no other. . . .[12]

A few years later, in 1892, the Court upheld powers delegated to the president to change important duties. In doing so, the majority declared "That Congress cannot delegate legislative power to the President is a principle universally recognized as vital to the integrity and maintenance of the system of government ordained by the Constitution." [13] Having made this point, the Court satisfied itself that the power to change import duties was not legislative power.

The doctrine of separation came into conflict with the demands

[12] *Kilbourne v. Thompson*, 103 US 168 (1881).
[13] *Field v. Clark*, 143 US 649 (1892).

of modern policymaking long ago. The Court, through semantic flights of fancy, seemed content to satisfy itself with strong statements about the theoretical impossibility of delegation, while in the same decisions upholding the impossible. The Court began to take a less ambiguous approach in the 1930s when it held that, under certain circumstances, Congress might find it necessary to delegate authority. Still, these powers were to be limited by congressional standards. "Congress cannot delegate any part of its legislative power except under the limitation of a prescribed standard," wrote the justices in 1931.[14]

The question of standards did not erect any important barriers to delegation. Acceptable standards were as vague and ill defined as such statements as "the public interest" and "fair and equitable allocation." Within a few years, the Court came very close to admitting that, in certain circumstances, no standard at all was necessary. In a 1947 decision, the Court wrote that it might have been desirable to have written explicit standards in the Home Owners Act of 1933, but it acknowledged that the existence of standards in this field perhaps was not really crucial. In such a highly developed and professionalized field as corporate management the Court reasoned, "experience and many precedents have crystallized into well-known and generally acceptable standards." [15] Therefore Congress did not have to write standards into the legislation in this case.

At various times, certain portions of the Federal Trade Commission Act were tested on the grounds that they were unconstitutional delegations. A court of appeals held that similar delegations had been upheld in the past and found no reason to hold these unconstitutional.[16]

The policymaking powers of regulatory commissions such as the Federal Trade Commission have caused some special problems

[14] *United States v. Chicago, Minneapolis and St. Paul Railroad Company,* 282 US 311, 324 (1931).
[15] *Fahey v. Mallonee,* 332 US 245, 250 (1947).
[16] *Sears, Roebuck and Company v. Federal Trade Commission,* 258 Fed. 307 (CCA 7 1918).

of control. Congress, anxious to keep the commissions under surveillance, was reluctant to give the president as much influence over them as he had over his executive departments. Consequently, the commissions were assigned to a kind of no man's land between the executive agencies and Congress. Their unusual status led to the use of the term "independent" in describing their relationship to both Congress and the chief executive.

The history of the commissions has been one of debate and political struggle between those who argue that the president should have more power over commissions and those who wish to strengthen congressional control. The presidential backers argue that the president is responsible for seeing that the law is faithfully executed and that independent commissions make this responsibility difficult, if not impossible, to carry out. Others cite the broad delegated powers enjoyed by the commissions and argue that Congress, as the source of these powers, should keep close watch over their use. Over the past 50 years, the presidential power advocates seem to have won a few victories, but the residency of the commissions in their no man's land remains unaffected.

William L. Cary, former chairman of the Securities and Exchange Commission, claims there can be very little difference between an executive agency and a regulatory commission in terms of its relationship to the president or Congress. He says that some executive agencies, like the Army Corps of Engineers, are closer to Congress than to the president even though scrutiny of an organization chart would seem to reveal the opposite. Influence over the commissions depends to a considerable extent on personalities within the congressional-interest groups-executive branch subsystem and the nature of the issue involved. Cary reflected the frustration of those caught between Congress and the president when he wrote, after his retirement:

> Government regulatory commissions are often referred to as "independent" agencies, but this cannot be taken at face value by anyone who has ever had any experience in Washington. In fact, government regulatory agencies are stepchildren whose custody is contested by

both Congress and the Executive, but without very much affection from either one.[17]

CHANGE IN EMPHASIS AT THE FTC

Congressional and presidential concern over government antitrust policy failed to lead to vigorous action by the Federal Trade Commission. Immediately after its establishment, the FTC encountered difficulties in enforcing those laws within its jurisdiction. The major problem which faced the FTC in its early years was the narrow interpretation that the Supreme Court gave to its enabling legislation. A member and one-time chairman of the commission wrote that in the first ten years the Supreme Court rent the commission's garment.[18] He thought the commission had made serious and thoughtful attempts to determine what it could and should prevent. The courts were not impressed with this thoughtfulness, and the FTC's powers were seriously limited in four cases decided soon after it had been established by Congress.[19]

The courts also narrowly defined the Federal Trade Commission's jurisdiction over unfair trade practices. When the commission acted to prevent misleading advertising for an obesity cure called Marvola, the Supreme Court objected. The FTC directed the producers of this substance to include in their advertising the statement that Marvola could not be safely taken without the supervision of a competent physician. After reviewing medical testimony, the Court held that the question of safety was one of opinion and not one of fact. The Court said that since the advertisers testified that they honestly believed their product to be safe, the FTC would

[17] William L. Cary, *Politics and the Regulatory Agencies* (New York: McGraw-Hill, 1967), p. 4.

[18] Nelson B. Gaskill, *The Regulaton of Competition* (New York: Harper and Brothers, 1936).

[19] *Federal Trade Commission v. Warren, Jones and Gratz*, 253 US 421 (1920); *Federal Trade Commission v. Curtis Publishing Company*, 260 US 568 (1923); *Federal Trade Commission v. Klesner*, 280 US 19 (1929); *Federal Trade Commission v. Raladam*, 283 US 643 (1931).

have to prove with scientific evidence that the product was harmful before it could act. Any question about the safety of a product, therefore, was resolved in favor of the producer. In an earlier case, the Court had weakened even more substantially the powers of the commission. According to the Court, the FTC's jurisdiction over unfair trade practices was limited to instances where a party injured or impaired the business of a competitor.[20] This left the commission without the power to move against a company that injured consumers through harmful or deceptive practices. Consumer protection was wrested, almost in its entirety, from the FTC by this decision; the consumer had no grounds upon which he could bring a complaint.

By 1938, sufficient momentum had been generated in Congress to expand the jurisdiction of the Federal Trade Commission to include consumer protection. The Wheeler-Lea Act of that year specifically empowered the commission to deal with "unfair or deceptive acts or practices in commerce." It contained provisions extending the commission's powers to dealing with false advertising of foods, drugs, devices, and cosmetics. With the Wheeler-Lea Act, the FTC began to devote most of its energies to the elimination of deception, particularly deception in advertising. Its antitrust activity subsided precipitously.

When the Surgeon General's report appeared in 1964, the Federal Trade Commission had had a substantial amount of experience with misleading advertising, including cigarette advertising. It had refined its regulatory techniques considerably over the years. A court decision had upheld the commission's right to demand positive disclosure of information where the effect of nondisclosure was to deceive a substantial segment of the purchasing public.[21]

Yet even with this experience and the necessary legal authority, all was not well with the Federal Trade Commission and its regulation of cigarette advertising. Cigarette consumption was rising rap-

---

[20] *Silver v. Federal Trade Commission,* 292 F. 752 (1923).

[21] P. *Lorillard Company v. Federal Trade Commission,* 186 F. 2d 52.58 (4th Cir. 1950).

idly. Policing advertisements had apparently not resulted in conveying to the public the health dangers involved in cigarette smoking. The commission was coming around to the view that in the face of all the adverse health reports, it was cigarette advertising alone that accounted for the rise in sales. Some of the commissioners had concluded that the public was being deceived into thinking that the consequences of smoking were social status and popularity rather than ill health. They felt that FTC actions against cigarette ads were not productive and, at the same time, that the commission should be able to use its powers over deceptive trade practices to stop whatever parts of advertisements were misleading the public.

Ironically, the root of the Federal Trade Commission's problem was substantially the same as the government's under the Sherman Act over half a century earlier. It was a procedural difficulty as much as anything else. The commission was attempting to regulate cigarette advertising on a case-by-case basis. Each time the commission ruled a particular advertisement deceptive, the industry came up with a variation that could squeak by under the rule of the previous case. This was proving to be an endless and fruitless process. The commission needed to write general regulations for the whole industry; the case method, whether employed by an agency or by the courts, was proving to be too cumbersome a method of developing regulatory policy.

In 1963, the commission moved to solve its problem by incorporating in its rules a procedure that could be used to write enforceable regulations for a whole category of industries. The chairman of the FTC saw the adoption of rulemaking procedures as the only way to make the commission an effective regulator. The Surgeon General's report gave the commission the impetus and the substantive information it needed to use its new rulemaking procedure in the field of cigarette advertising. This new procedure was set into motion one week after the Surgeon General released his report on smoking and health.

5

PROCEDURES USED
IN ADMINISTRATIVE
POLICYMAKING

Although the agencies of government are pictured in organization charts as arms of the executive, they derive their power from acts of Congress. Two types of power are granted by Congress: rulemaking and adjudicatory authority. Although the two powers are often indistinguishable because of functional overlap and mutual support, adjudicatory authority is frequently referred to as quasi-judicial in nature, while rulemaking is characterized as quasi-legislative or sub-legislative. As a practical method of distinguishing these powers from each other, one may think of adjudicatory actions as being used to perform judicial or courtlike activities, while rulemaking activities serve to develop policies in a manner comparable to that used by legislatures.

Since judicial decisions frequently have the same effect as legislative acts, it is sometimes difficult to distinguish between rulemaking and adjudicatory powers. Courts engage in rulemaking and adjudication simultaneously, as recent Supreme Court decisions in school desegregation and reapportionment have dramatically illustrated. Legislative and judicial policymaking differ partly because of the way a decision is made and partly because of the scope or applicability of the decision itself. Rulemaking is characterized by its general applicability. Rules formulated by agencies uniformly affect all within a given category, such as all cigarette producers. In contrast, adjudicatory action is based on a specific case involving an individual, partnership, or corporation. The end result of an adjudicatory proceeding is a determination whether or not those named in the suit have violated a law or rule, or perhaps whether the parties in question qualify for a license of some kind. Once the adjudicatory decision is made, a precedent is established that may apply to others similarly situated. Consequently, adjudication—as well as rulemaking—can have a broad impact on society or general policy.

The difference between these two types of power is of more than passing interest.[1] Each has its own procedural advantages and disadvantages. When an agency acts in its adjudicatory capacity, it must use procedures that are more formal and more carefully developed than those employed under its rulemaking functions. Adjudicatory procedures in agencies are very similar to the procedures and practices used in a courtroom. Rulemaking procedures, on the other hand, are usually much less formal. In some cases, agency rulemaking procedures are less formal than those used to govern university senate meetings. At times they are similar to the procedures, or absence of procedures, used by moderators of round-table discussions. The different degree of formality of the procedures is largely determined by the expected impact of the rule under con-

[1] For a detailed discussion of the differences between rulemaking and adjudication see: David L. Shapiro, "The Choice of Rulemaking or Adjudication in the Development of Administrative Policy," 78 *Harvard Law Review* 921 (1965).

sideration. In agency rulemaking, it is incumbent upon the agency itself to determine which issues require formal rulemaking procedures and which do not. The more formal procedures require that the public be notified and be given the opportunity to be heard. They are patterned after those used when congressional committees hold public hearings and call witnesses to testify.

ADJUDICATION AND RULEMAKING AT THE FTC

The Federal Trade Commission now uses both adjudicatory and rulemaking powers to enforce and implement the laws within its jurisdiction, although for many years it used rulemaking powers only in certain very narrowly defined areas, such as the labeling of fur products. The adjudicatory procedure that the commission frequently uses may be initiated through a complaint filed by someone who considers himself aggrieved by a violation of one of the laws within the commission's jurisdiction. The complaint is followed by a formal hearing, usually before a hearing examiner, designed to assure the accused party of many of the protections he would be provided if he were a defendant in court. If the examiner decides there has been a violation, he can recommend that a cease and desist order be issued. The defendant then has the opportunity to appeal, first to the commissioners themselves and, should that fail, he may attempt to make an appeal to a United States Court of Appeals. As a result of its ruling, the commission has the power to levy fines up to $5,000 per day if the offense continues.

Although adjudicatory and rulemaking procedures are the most powerful devices at the command of the commission, they are not the most frequently used. Rulemaking was utilized very sparingly until the commission rewrote its own operating procedures in 1963, and adjudicatory proceedings are initiated in cases of blatant industrial violations, and then only when everything else has failed. Most of the Federal Trade Commission's efforts over the years have been directed toward gaining voluntary compliance or informal agreement. This practice is comparable to settling matters out of court and has the same virtues: expediency, less complexity, and lower costs; but is also fraught with similar disadvantages. No formal record is made to guide others and neither party in the dispute is protected by the rights and practices of legal proceedings.

The Federal Trade Commission uses three techniques to secure voluntary compliance with the law. One device is the advisory opinion. In the federal judicial system, unlike those of other countries and some of the states, the courts will not tell a party whether or not something it plans to do might be illegal. Courts will decide only cases and controversies at law. However, the bureaucracy is not so limited. Given the complexities of modern government, it is fortunate that the bureaucracy is free to tell an interested party how it might view some proposed action. Industry frequently requests opinions from the Federal Trade Commission, and the commissioners respond but note that their opinions are only advisory and not binding on the government. The advisory opinion is a useful device and it is so popular that it accounts for a large part of the growth of quasi-judicial functions of agencies.

When the Federal Trade Commission wants to reach a broad spectrum of the corporate world, it resorts to another informal device called the Trade Practices Conference. The commission invites industry to these conferences to discuss with the commissioners their regulatory problems and, it is hoped, everyone leaves the conference with his problems solved. Occasionally, voluntary codes or voluntary trade practice rules come out of these meetings.

The third kind of informal procedure leads to what are known as consent orders. These are voluntary agreements reached by the commission and a party about to enter, or in the course of, an adjudicatory proceeding. In the case of the consent order, the Federal Trade Commission has some leverage to exert over an accused business or corporation. By signing a consent order, the party involved in the proceeding agrees to stop whatever he was doing that the commission thought suspect, and the commission agrees to drop the proceedings. Signing the consent order is not an admission of guilt. The pressure that the commission can apply to sign an order—especially to a small company, which might find it could ill afford the time or cash required to fight the commission or the publicity that would result—has made the consent order procedure one that receives much criticism.

The informal procedures and adjudicatory procedures are a languid regulatory stick for the commission. General rulemaking is, in many ways, a much more potent device, but there have been powerful pressures on the commission not to use this procedure. And, of course, there was some question—articulated by industrial groups such as the cigarette producers—as to whether the legal authority to exercise general rulemaking powers was delegated to the Federal Trade Commission.

THE FEDERAL TRADE COMMISSION'S EXPERIENCE WITH CIGARETTE REGULATION

The limited effectiveness of the commission's policymaking procedures is evident in the FTC's record on cigarette advertising regulation. The commission had invoked its adjudicatory powers in cases involving cigarette producers approximately 25 times between 1938 and 1968. Although most of these cases were settled by consent orders, some did result in cease and desist orders. In dealing with an industry-wide problem such as deceptive cigarette advertising on a case-by-case basis, the Federal Trade Commission found itself faced with problems not much different from those that the courts encountered when they attempted to make broad policies on a case-by-case basis. Discovery of the inadequacies of the case approach in the courts was one of the prime reasons for establishing the commission in 1914. Ironically, nearly 50 years later, the commission was attempting to act in a manner similar to that found ineffective by the courts.

The insufficiencies of the case approach stem from the fact that the judgment or order in each case applies only to the parties to the case. Others who might be engaged in the same deceptive act, or one closely related, are not immediately affected by the commission's decision involving their less fortunate brethren. It is possible for those not named as a party to the case to continue the "illegal" practice until the Federal Trade Commission moves against them. This can take months or even years. Furthermore, only activities or practices complained of in the suit can be prohibited by the decision; slight variations from that practice even by the same parties must be dealt with by separate decisions.

In the case of cigarette advertising, the commission found itself putting out brush fires of deception while the inferno raged on. There was no way for the commission to state authoritatively a general policy of what constituted deception in cigarette ads for all advertisers. The procedures employed in adjudicatory actions narrowly define the scope of admissible evidence. Discussion of the ramifications of an industry-wide problem is difficult under such circumstances. Then too, the commission's action against cigarette producers only provided requirements about what *could not* be done, but not about what *had to* be done. That is, the Federal Trade Commission could not require that a health warning appear on all packages through its adjudicatory procedures. The only way it could have approached this requirement would have been to ask the manufacturers to do this voluntarily or deal with the cigarette companies one at a time through cases that, in each instance, would have had to prove that such a positive disclosure was necessary.

One of the early cases involving cigarette advertising points up the difficulties in commission procedures. The manufacturers of a now extinct brand called Julep cigarettes claimed in their advertisements that their product was a remedy for coughs. Even in the early 1940s, this strained the credulity of the commission, and the Julep makers were forced to stop making the claim.[2] Yet within a short period, other makers advertised similar health claims. One producer proclaimed that there was not a cough in a carload of his cigarettes. That same manufacturer later announced that more doctors smoked his cigarettes than any other brand. Now, according to the FTC, manufacturers use subtle techniques for this purpose, as when

2 *Penn Tobacco Company*, 34 F.T.C. 1636 (1942).

they imply that a filter protects the smoker. Some examples of such innuendoes are, "the flavor of the world's finest tobaccos through the Kent filter" and "white filter flavor" (L & M).[3]

Since it was impossible to fight the health inferences and subtleties in cigarette ads through adjudicatory procedures, the best way to eliminate deception, according to the Federal Trade Commission, was to require that a positive health warning statement appear in each advertisement. Rulemaking authority was necessary before that requirement could be made. Commissioner Philip Elman summed up the FTC's frustration with adjudicatory procedures in the field of cigarette advertising and defended the effectiveness of rulemaking procedures. When the tobacco interests challenged the commission's authority to use rulemaking procedures, Commissioner Elman responded:

> Suppose there is a product in general use throughout the United States. . . . And suppose scientific research should conclusively establish that that product induced sterility. Would you say that under the Federal Trade Commission Act the only way in which this Commission could proceed to carry out its responsibilities of preventing deception . . . is to issue a complaint and a cease and desist order against each of the thousands and thousands of manufacturers? Or has Congress allowed us an alternative method of proceeding. . . ?[4]

The Federal Trade Commission did not rely on adjudicatory procedures alone but also attempted, without success, to deal with misleading cigarette advertising by informal means. In 1955, as a result of a Trade Practices Conference, the commission issued a set of cigarette advertising guidelines. These were used in an attempt to have cigarette manufacturers voluntarily refrain from advertising the levels of tar and nicotine contained in their cigarettes. The guidelines brought an end to the "tar derby" when the manufactur-

---

[3] *Report to Congress*, Federal Trade Commission, June 30, 1968, p. 20 (mimeo.).

[4] Hearings before the F.T.C. on Cigarette Labeling and Advertising, Vol. VII, March 16, 1964, p. 61 (typewritten).

ers agreed to discontinue advertisements containing confusing and ambiguous claims about the tar and nicotine content of their product. Other parts of the voluntary guidelines worked unsuccessfully because the FTC was powerless to enforce them.

In 1966, in light of growing public and congressional interest in the possible health implications of tar and nicotine, the Federal Trade Commission reversed itself and notified cigarette manufacturers that they were at liberty to advertise tar and nicotine levels, provided they made no health claims with respect to them. A year later, after standardized measurement techniques had been agreed upon, the commission announced the opening of a smoking laboratory to measure these levels. It began to publish the measurements for all cigarette brands periodically and requested that Congress require these measurements to be printed on cigarette packages and appear in advertising.

Congress ignored this recommendation, and the law that required a health warning on packages prevented the commission from making a further package requirement on its own. However, in the summer of 1970, the commission proposed to issue a trade regulation rule requiring the tar-nicotine information to appear in all cigarette advertising. By the end of the year the cigarette manufacturers agreed among themselves to do this, and the commission approved the agreement and dropped its proposal. This agreement, although voluntary, like the 1955 guidelines, was stronger because the FTC, through its newly adopted trade regulation rule procedure, claimed the power to enforce the agreement if necessary.

THE FEDERAL TRADE COMMISSION ADOPTS RULEMAKING PROCEDURES

One of the factors leading to the report of the Surgeon General's Advisory Committee on Smoking and Health was that some individuals outside the Federal Trade Commission also began to realize that without rulemaking powers, the commission could not hope to effectively warn the public of the health hazards of smoking.

In April 1962, Senator Neuberger wrote a letter to Paul Rand Dixon, the newly appointed chairman of the Federal Trade Commission, suggesting that any cigarette advertisement that failed to carry a health warning was inherently deceptive. She asked why the FTC could not adopt this position officially and subsequently require that all cigarette advertising carry a health warning. The answer to Senator Neuberger's inquiry was that the commission had never adopted the necessary rulemaking procedures to do what she suggested. None of the informal or adjudicatory procedures that the FTC had been using could have accomplished what the senator was suggesting.

Senator Neuberger's letter found a responsive ear within the commission, however. When Chairman Dixon came to the Federal Trade Commission in 1961, he began, almost immediately, to push for the use of general rulemaking powers. He saw the incorporation of rulemaking as an important means to strengthen what was a rather ineffective regulatory process. Plans for the adoption of rulemaking procedures were already in the works when the chairman answered Senator Neuberger's letter. His response hinted openly that the only major obstacle to the adoption of the Neuberger suggestion was the gathering of substantial evidence establishing a direct relationship between smoking and ill health:

> If the Commission is able to secure competent probative scientific evidence including that furnished by the Public Health Service, that a causal relationship exists between cigarette smoking and lung cancer, heart ailments, etc., it is likely that an order of the Commission, based on such evidence, which required an affirmative disclosure of the possible hazards to health from smoking cigarettes, would be upheld in the appellate courts.[5]

One might have assumed, as the cigarette people did, that the Federal Trade Commission was preparing itself for the report of the Surgeon General's Advisory Committee. The FTC announced the adoption of general rulemaking procedures in June 1962, at about

[5] Quoted in Maurine B. Neuberger, *Smoke Screen: Tobacco and the Public Welfare* (Englewood Cliffs, N.J.: Prentice-Hall, 1963), p. 58.

the same time the Surgeon General set up his Advisory Committee.

Although the adoption of rulemaking procedures was probably coincidental to the cigarette controversy, the commission busied itself issuing trade regulation rules (the official name given the end product of the new rulemaking procedure) for uncontroversial products as if it might have been practicing for its cigarette rule. The first rule was issued in mid-1963 while the Surgeon General's committee was preparing its report. It concerned the size of sleeping bags. A few months later another rule was issued concerning the use of the term *leakproof* or *guaranteed leakproof* in advertising dry cell batteries. Another prohibited misbranding leather belts. None of the three trade regulation rules stirred much controversy; they were promulgated practically without popular notice. The fourth rulemaking attempt was, however, destined to stir more public reaction than the Federal Trade Commission had anticipated or desired. The cigarette makers, who were next to be affected by a trade regulation rule, were determined to prove that the FTC had no authority to write such rules. Had they succeeded, they would have had a double victory: the cigarette rule would have been quashed, and the commission would have remained a weakened watchdog of the public interest, confined to either its informal or its case method of regulation.

Use of the new trade regulation rule procedure in the cigarette labeling controversy provided almost the only positive note for the FTC when, in the late 1960s, two very critical studies of the commission appeared. One of these was written for the American Bar Association by a committee chaired by Miles W. Kirkpatrick, later appointed chairman of the commission by President Nixon, and the other by a group of law school students working for Ralph Nader during their summer recess. The latter report contained this statement: "The singularly unusual case of the FTC's action on deceptive cigarette advertising is indicative of what the FTC would be capable of if properly directed and motivated." [6]

6 Edward F. Cox, Robert C. Fellmeth, and John E. Schulz, *The Nader Report on the Federal Trade Commission* (New York: Grove Press, 1969), p. 77. The American Bar Association report was released on September 16, 1969.

The commission's actions on cigarettes resulting from the adoption of the trade regulation rule procedure counted for a great deal in the eyes of the FTC's critics. Something which seemed to escape their scrutiny was the blow which Congress dealt to the FTC as a result of and immediately following its actions on cigarettes. There was good evidence that Congress liked best the image of the commission as the "little old lady of Pennsylvania Avenue." When the lady got tough her congressional sponsors tried to remove her tennis shoes and put her back in the rocking chair. As the FTC has become more aggressive over the past few years it has had the backing of a Congress increasingly interested in consumer affairs. Congress exerts considerable influence over the regulatory commissions; often the aggressiveness or lack of it in the commissions is a reflection of congressional attitudes toward regulation.

What Congress did not do in the cigarette controversy, the U.S. District Court did in April 1972. The court's ruling prohibited the FTC from requiring the display of octane ratings on gasoline pumps and stripped the commission of the rulemaking power it had carefully developed during the early 1960s. Had this decision held, the commission would have been forced to operate as it had since 1914, on a case-by-case basis. The Court of Appeals reversed the lower court decision and the Supreme Court refused to review the case. Therefore, the FTC's rulemaking powers remained intact.[7] The commission's supporters in Congress came to its defense with legislation that would have explicitly granted the FTC rulemaking powers. The bills became unnecessary with the Court of Appeals decision.[8]

A lengthy summary of the report was published that day in the *New York Times*. Practically the only complimentary comment for the commission was the notation of the adoption of the new procedure: "To place our criticism in perspective, we wish to emphasize that recent years have witnessed an improvement in several aspects of the FTC's operations. The FTC has sought to improve its rules of practice and procedure. It has experimented with new administrative techniques such as the trade regulation rule. . . ."

[7] National Petroleum Refiners Association v. Federal Trade Commission, 482 F.2d 672 (D.C. Cir. 1973).

[8] The provisions were included in the consumer protection bill introduced

According to the Federal Trade Commission's amended manual, trade regulation rules "cover all applications of a particular statutory provision, may be nationwide in effect, or may be limited to particular areas or industries or to particular products or geographical areas. . . ." Trade regulation rules give the FTC the capability of issuing formal rules or guides to govern the conduct of large categories of producers. And once the rules are issued, any violation of them could be used to initiate adjudicatory proceedings.

The commissioners themselves by majority vote decide whether or not to initiate rulemaking procedures. Citizens or groups may petition the Federal Trade Commission to commence a proceeding but the commission itself decides whether or not the petition should be acted upon. The proceeding on the cigarette labeling and advertising rule was initiated by the commission.

Ordinarily, the commissioners rely upon the Division of Trade Regulation Rules, an office within the FTC, to write the draft rule and arrange for and conduct preliminary hearings.[9] The cigarette labeling rule was no ordinary rule, however. The commissioners decided to handle this matter by themselves and they prepared for it carefully.

The Federal Trade Commission followed the progress of the Surgeon General's Advisory Committee by appointing a liaison man who attended most of the open meetings of the committee. Several months before the Surgeon General was to issue his report, the Federal Trade Commission organized within its staff a special task force on cigarettes consisting of physicians, economists, and attorneys. When the report was issued, the commission was ready to move; within one week the Federal Trade Commission issued a notice that it planned to begin a rulemaking proceeding.

Rulemaking by administrative agencies should take place in public, not in the privacy of a bureaucrat's office. Rules made by agencies are as powerful and binding as acts of legislatures and, in

---

in the Senate by Senator Warren Magnuson (S. 356, January 12, 1973) and Congressman John E. Moss (HR 20, January 3, 1973).

[9] The division was established in 1962 when the commission's rules were amended to include the trade regulation rule procedure.

a democracy, citizens should be provided with the opportunity to participate in the formulation of policies that affect their lives. Elections expose legislators to public pressures; administrative agencies are insulated from the electoral process and perhaps from responding to the public. Somehow citizen participation should be built into the administrative policymaking process to enhance the system's conformity with theories of representative government. Among the techniques that can be used to build fairness into the administrative process is the adoption of procedures similar to those used in judicial proceedings; participation in the administrative process can be encouraged through public hearings like those before committees of Congress.

THE ADMINISTRATIVE PROCEDURE ACT

Demands to adopt court-like procedures for administrative agencies came from such quarters as the American Bar Association in the early 1930s. The expansion of government activity during the New Deal sounded the alarm for many who were genuinely concerned about the infringement of fundamental rights that individuals might suffer at the hands of irresponsible bureaucrats. Others sought simply to curb the regulatory powers of government over business and industry. Pressures for the adoption of stricter, more uniform administrative procedures were delayed by World War II, but were revived shortly after the end of the war. In 1946, Congress passed the Administrative Procedure Act (APA),[10] which sets out procedures to be followed by agencies when they engage in rulemaking and adjudicatory proceedings. The procedures have some relationship to those used by courts, although they are not quite as formal or as carefully stated. Furthermore, certain elements of congressional hearing procedures are also incorporated in the act. There are several exemptions from the requirements of the act, recogni-

[10] 60 Stat. 237 (1946). In 1966, the act was incorporated in Title 5 of the *United States Code*. The *Code* is supplemented annually and revised every six years.

tion of the fact that there are large numbers of agency problems that could not be effectively handled under these formal procedures.

If every policymaking action of an agency were to be treated as a judicial proceeding or a legislative hearing, the decision-making process would grind to a halt. So the first difficulty faced by those who wrote the Administrative Procedure Act was to decide which agency actions the act covered and which it did not. All military and foreign affairs functions are exempt from its requirements. Also exempt are "any matters relating to agency management or personnel or to public property, loans, grants, benefits, or contracts." The act then goes on to differentiate between rulemaking, or quasi-legislative functions, and the adjudicatory functions of agencies. The most formal procedures in the act apply to all adjudicatory functions, but to only some agency rulemaking functions. There is a distinction made in the act between *formal* and *informal* rulemaking.

In formal rulemaking, only some of the required adjudicatory procedures are employed; for example, hearings are conducted, a public record is kept, and certain rules of evidence are followed. However, the most important difference between the formal and informal processes is that in the former a public hearing is required and in the latter, the decision as to whether or not to hold a hearing is left up to the agency. How does an agency know when it must hold a public hearing? A hearing is required only when the legislation under which the agency operates requires it. There are only a few statutes that require formal hearings for all rulemaking; in fact, none of the 11 major acts that the Federal Trade Commission administers require hearings in rulemaking. When agencies are not required by legislation to hold a hearing, the rulemaking section of the Administrative Procedure Act is followed only if the agency decides it should be followed.[11]

---

[11] The rulemaking section of the Administrative Procedure Act states that requirements for notice and hearing need not be followed ". . . in any situation in which the agency for good cause finds . . . that notice and public procedure . . . are impracticable, unnecessary, or contrary to the public interest." Of course, the courts could declare invalid any rule made if an agency acted arbi-

In formal rulemaking, or when an agency elects to do so, the Administrative Procedure Act requires that a public notice of rulemaking be given including: (1) a statement of time, place, and nature of the proceedings (also giving details of plans for a hearing if one is to be held); (2) reference to the authority under which the rule is proposed; (3) the terms and substance of the proposed rule. The APA goes on to say that those affected by a proposed rule must be given time to respond in writing. Thirty days' notice has to be given before a rule becomes effective, and interested persons have the right to petition for amendment or repeal.

Frequently agencies elect to use these formal rulemaking procedures even when they are not required, particularly when the rule will affect large numbers or groups of individuals. There are several reasons for favoring the formal process, not the least of which is the practical matter of enlisting support for the rule. If those affected by a rule participate in its formulation, chances are they will better understand its provisions and the rationale behind it. This is no guarantee of support for the measure, but it should be an easier rule to enforce than one made behind the closed doors of a bureau chief's office.

In all of its rulemaking, the Federal Trade Commission has followed formal procedures. The commissioners never seriously considered adopting the cigarette labeling and advertising rule without holding a formal hearing because they sensed how controversial their proposal was. They knew that if they adopted the rule without hearings, the cigarette manufacturers could seize upon the secretiveness of their action to argue that the FTC was undemocratic, arbitrary and dangerous. To protect itself from such accusations, and with genuine interest in determining if anyone had sound arguments for rejecting their proposed rule, the commission set in motion the procedural machinery described in the Administrative Procedure Act for formal rulemaking.

---

trarily or capriciously in failing to give notice of rulemaking and/or failing to hold hearings.

THE FEDERAL REGISTER

The first step taken was to give notice to interested parties. Although not required to do so, the commission mailed a letter of its intentions to those it presumed would be interested. And it released a news item to the press. Simultaneously, it placed a notice in the official publication of the executive branch, the *Federal Register,* an action required by the Administrative Procedure Act in all rulemaking activities.

The *Federal Register* brought some order to inexcusable administrative chaos that existed before its publication in 1936. Prior to that year, there was no single published document containing the official actions of agencies including rules or adjudicatory decisions. There was no effective way for the government to communicate with its constituents about the actions taken by administrators. There was no good way, save contacting each agency separately, for the public to know what decisions agencies were making and how they changed the law. As the quantity of administrative decisions grew, it became literally impossible for the left hand of the bureaucracy to know what the right hand was doing. The resultant disorders were bad, not only for administrative effectiveness, but also for the citizen who had little information about what his government was doing.

The need for an official publication containing administrative actions came forcefully to the attention of the public in 1935 in an important and critical Supreme Court decision.[12] The Court, in striking down the National Recovery Act, noted that enforcement officials of the administration, industrialists, and the lower courts had not been informed that certain administrative regulations promulgated under the act had been revoked. Some of the worst fears of the legal community were confirmed in this case of ill use of administrative policymaking powers. This failure of the administration prompted Congress to pass the Federal Register Act in 1935, the same year the Court handed down its decision.

[12] *Panama Refining Company v. Ryan,* 293 US 388 (1935).

The Federal Register Act requires that all documents having general applicability and legal effect must be published in the *Register*. This includes such items as general statements of agency powers and procedures and copies of the forms it uses for applications and other purposes. The Administrative Procedure Act spells out those actions of agencies that must be published. It states, for example, that notice of proposed rulemaking shall be published in the *Federal Register*. Accordingly, the Federal Trade Commission published in the *Register* a notice of rulemaking proceedings for the establishment of trade regulation rules for the advertising and labeling of cigarettes. The notice contained a draft of the proposed rule, an explanation of the legal authority upon which the action was to be taken, and the dates for hearings before the commission. The public was also informed in the notice that they could file written data, views, or arguments concerning the rule or the subject of the proceeding in general. In the notice, the commission announced that a public hearing on the rule would begin at 10 A.M., Monday, March 16, 1964. The announcement was published in the *Federal Register* two full months before the hearing was scheduled to begin.[13]

The Federal Trade Commission makes it a practice not to rely exclusively on the *Register* for dissemination of information concerning its rulemaking proposals. Copies of the cigarette notice were mailed to a large number of companies, associations, and individuals who might conceivably have had some interest in the proceedings. Furthermore, shortly after the notice was placed in the *Register*, the Federal Trade Commission directly solicited statements from state and local health officers and associations, physicians, med-

[13] The Office of the Federal Register is a part of the National Archives of the United States. It publishes the *Register* daily, Tuesday through Saturday, and places the *Register* in the mails before 9 A.M. the day it is published. It is then delivered at no charge to the courts, executive agencies, and to members of Congress. Copies are mailed to lawyers, representatives of special interest groups, and other interested parties. These individuals subscribe to the *Register* for $25 per year. In 1972, there were approximately 17,000 paid subscribers, and over 10,000 additional copies were distributed free of charge.

ical scientists, behavioral scientists, chemists, cigarette manufacturers, and many others.

The response to the notice of proposed rulemaking was substantial. Several individuals and groups asked that they be scheduled for oral testimony at the hearings; others submitted lengthy statements. Still others wrote brief letters stating their position. A large number of unsolicited letters and petitions were received by the commission. Some of these came from high school students who had been recently subjected to antismoking movies, others from gratified parents looking for official support in their private campaigns to keep cigarettes from their children.

All of the communications were placed in the public record of the hearing. They were available to anyone who wanted to read them before, after, or during the commission hearings.

When the hearings began, the commissioners were fortified with staff documents and prepared statements in much the same way a congressional committee is prepared for a hearing on proposed legislation. The draft of the rule had been widely circulated, perhaps even more widely circulated than proposed legislation might have been. Comments had been received from a sizeable cross section of the public, and the commissioners were prepared to hear witnesses discuss the feasibility and wisdom of the proposed health warning for cigarette packages and advertising.

6

THE RULEMAKING HEARINGS

Witnesses and spectators at Federal Trade Commission hearings sit in a large, impressive, wood-paneled room that resembles both a congressional hearing room and a courtroom. The focal point of the chamber is a raised bench, behind which are velvet draperies that serve as a backdrop for the elegantly upholstered swivel chairs of the five commissioners. There are counsel tables in front of the bench, a small table for the official recorder, and a lectern on which witnesses may rest their notes and elbows. A railing separates the hard wooden spectator pews from the seats of the staff and those who are participating in the hearing.

On March 16, 1964, the commissioners took their seats in front of the long, blue velvet draperies to begin three consecutive days of hearings on the cigarette labeling and advertising rule. The proposed rule, which had been circulated well in advance of the hearing, contained three major sections. The first was the requirement that a health warning appear in all advertising and on cigarette packages. Drafts of two warning statements, either of which would have satisfied the Federal Trade Commission, were also in the first section:

a. CAUTION—CIGARETTE SMOKING IS A HEALTH HAZARD: The Surgeon General's Advisory Committee has found that "cigarette smoking contributes to mortality from specific diseases and to the overall death rate";

or

b. CAUTION: Cigarette smoking is dangerous to health. It may cause death from cancer and other diseases.

Another section of the rule attempted to reach the more subtle implications of cigarette advertising by banning "words, pictures, symbols, sounds, devices or demonstrations, or any combination thereof that would lead the public to believe cigarette smoking promotes good health or physical well-being."

The FTC was to find itself overruled by Congress on half of its proposal. The label was to be required only on packages, not in advertising. The ban on radio and television ads came much later, and when it came it was by an act of Congress not the FTC or the FCC. The requirement for inclusion of the health warning in all printed advertising also came later. It was the result of a voluntary agreement between the commission and the manufacturers, made in 1972 after a congressional ban on commission action against forcing such a requirement was expiring.

CIGARETTE HEARINGS
AT THE FEDERAL TRADE COMMISSION

Hearings themselves serve some useful and important purposes. However, one of these purposes does not seem to be changing the viewpoints of any of the participants. The hearings do provide an opportunity to make a public record on the issue and to communicate views among those involved in a controversy. Such a hearing is likely to facilitate subsequent enforcement and public acceptance of the agency action. In some highly complex technical matters, agency hearings provide useful, factual information that the staff has not been able to find elsewhere. With the considerable amount of time that went into the preparation of the cigarette labeling case, however, there was little factual information that the commissioners did not have at their disposal. Backed by the scientific evidence of the Surgeon General's report and the detailed legal work of their counsel's office, the commissioners seemed fairly certain as to what the outcome of the hearings would be. Chairman Paul Rand Dixon had some doubts about the wisdom of confronting the powerful cigarette industry while the Federal Trade Commission's new rulemaking procedures might be vulnerable. He was anxious to expand the use of the rulemaking device in commission activities, but as an experienced chief investigator for a congressional committee during the Kefauver drug investigation, he was politically sensitive to the pitfalls of consumer regulation.

Three commissioners, John Reilly, Mary Gardiner Jones, and Philip Elman were in favor of the rule as the Federal Trade Commission had drafted it. Commissioner Reilly took no part in the questioning at the hearings. The active participation of Commissioner Elman apparently strengthened his support of the FTC's proposed rule. The tobacco interests' challenge to the commission's power to issue the ruling irked Elman. His interest in establishing the authority of the commission to act in the cigarette case seemed to grow stronger with the intensity of the tobacco interests' challenge.

Commissioner Everette A. MacIntyre, who had been with the Federal Trade Commission about 25 years, was not a strong supporter of the rule, yet he was not active in opposition to it. Regarded as the commission's expert on administrative law, he was cautious about infringing upon the powers of other agencies, particularly the Federal Communications Commission and its jurisdiction over radio and television advertising. Commissioner MacIntyre was more reluctant than the others to undertake any action that could have proved injurious to the tobacco economy, and after the other commissioners had adopted the proposed rule, he issued a separate statement of disagreement. (Some attributed this reluctance to the fact that he was a native of North Carolina.) He wrote that the wording of the health warning in both advertising and on packages should be left to negotiations that would follow further developments in the smoking and health field. He also suggested delaying the effective date six months to give all parties more adequate opportunity to work out an effective solution. Commissioner MacIntyre opposed the imposition of additional regulations on cigarette manufacturers in all of the Federal Trade Commission's reports to Congress during his tenure.

WITNESSES

The commissioners heard the testimony of 29 witnesses during three days of hearings. The unpublished record, available to the public at commission headquarters, is 538 pages long.[1] It would have been difficult for any observer to detect differences between what they were watching at the Federal Trade Commission and what they might have watched had they traveled a few hundred yards down Pennsylvania Avenue to the Capitol. Chairman Dixon opened the proceedings by inviting each witness to read or submit his statement for the record, and then the witness was asked to

[1] Federal Trade Commission, *Hearings on Trade Regulation Rule on Cigarette Labeling and Advertising*, D. 215-8-7, March 17, 1964 (typewritten).

answer questions of the commissioners. Some witnesses were asked no questions at all. The atmosphere of the hearing room was light and friendly toward those who testified in favor of the commission's proposal. When those who came to question the wisdom of the commission rose to testify, tension crept into the air. At times opponents were questioned closely, providing some of the same electric drama television viewers were occasionally exposed to while watching the Senate's controversial McCarthy or Kefauver committee hearings.

The order of appearance of witnesses at a hearing is a clue as to how those conducting the hearings are disposed toward the issue involved. Sympathetic witnesses are scheduled during prime time, which is generally early in each day, with the "prime" of the prime being early in the first day. These are the hours when interest is highest and the press is most alert to what is said. The whole tone of the hearings, at least in the public eye, can be governed by what happens first.

It was no accident that the Assistant Surgeon General of the Public Health Service was scheduled to appear first. He was followed by Senator Neuberger. Thus, the Federal Trade Commission began its hearings with two very strong statements in favor of its proposed rule. The third witness was from the Tobacco Institute, and he was followed by two university research scientists who favored the proposed rule.

The second day of the hearings saw marketing experts, scientists, representatives of advertising, and tobacco growers' associations testify. The third and final day was somewhat more unusual. It was politician's day at the commission. Governors of the tobacco states or their representatives and four members of the North Carolina congressional delegation testified. The appearance of congressmen before an administrative agency is an interesting reversal of roles. It is not unusual for a member of Congress to intervene with agencies on behalf of a constituent, but it is unusual for members to testify at an agency hearing, especially when trying to prevent the agency from acting. The appearance of this large a number of elected officials underscores the importance of agency policymaking activities. The commissioners listened patiently and courteously to the elected officials before them. There was little questioning, although some commissioners expressed skepticism that the proposed rule would bring as much economic and social damage as the witnesses claimed it would. Nevertheless, the commissioners understood that elected officials from the tobacco states really had no choice but to testify and vigorously protest a proposal such as this one, which so directly affected their constituents. The congressmen present similarly knew that they were not going to change the commissioners' views simply by testifying against the proposed rule. Instead, they hoped with the cigarette manufacturers to have the issue transferred from the commission to Congress. By the time the Federal Trade Commission announced that it was scheduling hearings, those who opposed the health warning requirement knew that congressional action would be one of the most effective ways, if not the only way, of halting the commission's proposal.

POSITION OF THE INDUSTRY

One tactic in the strategy to move the controversy to Congress required cigarette manufacturers to publicly ignore and downgrade the importance of the Federal Trade Commission by electing not to personally appear at its hearings. Instead, a lawyer from the prestigious Washington firm of Covington and Burling was retained by the Tobacco Institute to represent manufacturers at the hearings. The lawyer, H. Thomas Austern, chose to ignore the merits of the smoking and health controversy and instead concentrated on the position that the commission did not have general rulemaking powers. He insisted that the absence of these powers in the Federal Trade Commission legislation meant that the issue of a health warning requirement would have to be settled by Congress; furthermore, according to Mr. Austern, the issue was of too much importance to be decided by an administrative agency. The elected representatives of the people should decide this, he said. Mr.

Austern warned the commissioners that if they adopted the proposed rule, the Tobacco Institute would take the Federal Trade Commission to court to demonstrate that rulemaking powers were not delegated by Congress.

With this defense decided upon, the attorney for the Tobacco Institute was faced with the task of developing the legal arguments necessary to show that the commission was acting where it lacked the authority to do so. The major thrust of his argument was that if the members of Congress had intended that the commission formulate general rules under the Federal Trade Commission Act of 1914, they would have said so in the act itself. Austern pointed to other acts adminstered by the commission in which the delegation of rulemaking authority was made explicit. Section 8 of the Fur Products Labeling Act of 1945, for example, contains this statement: "The Commission is authorized and directed to prescribe rules and regulations governing the manner and form of disclosing information required by this Act. . . ." The commission's arguments, which are discussed more fully below, were that the delegation of rulemaking powers was both implicit and explicit in the act. Furthermore, since 1914, judicial interpretation and scholarly opinions of agency authority had pointed to the existence of this authority under the statute that created the Federal Trade Commission. The Tobacco Institute remained adamant in its position throughout the hearings, as was expected. Their opposition, although not well founded in prevailing opinions of the law, served to cast doubt on the commission's authority and to make it clear that, should the commission promulgate its proposed rule, there would be months of uncertainty as the issue was fought out in Congress, the courts, or both. Most lawyers would not have defended the Tobacco Institute's position if the debate had been strictly academic; the law on administrative rulemaking is quite clear and favorable to agency powers. Mr. Austern, however, was not engaging in an academic debate. His presentation served the very useful purpose for which it was designed. The commissioners knew now, if they had not known before, that their rule was due to be reviewed in places where the commission was not very influential.

THE COMMISSIONERS RESPOND

As the commissioners listened to Mr. Austern's testimony, it was evident that they were becoming increasingly irritated. Perhaps it was the realization that the powerful tobacco interests might succeed in altering or nullifying their new rulemaking procedure by persuading Congress to enact a law specifically removing their rulemaking power, or perhaps they were wearied by the thought of protracted argument in Congress and the courts on the cigarette labeling issue itself. At any rate, the commissioners were lawyers and they were not receptive to criticism of their action based on their alleged misinterpretation of the Federal Trade Commission's legal mandate.

The patience of the commissioners had worn thin by the second day of the hearings. Anxious to consider the substantive issues involved in the enforcement of their proposed rule, they were tired of defending their authority to act. When Gilbert H. Weil, a representative of the Association of National Advertisers, took up the Tobacco Institute's argument, he elicited this spirited response from Commissioner Elman:

> Lawyers apparently feel that all law is divided into either substantive or procedural, or legislative, executive, and judicial, and, therefore they have to talk in those terms. And a lot of lawyers apparently have not read what the Supreme Court and what other students of the administrative process have written on the nature of administrative rulemaking. I suggest you lawyers read these cases and come to us with a more realistic approach to the real problem, that we have here —instead of talking about fantasies and fictions.[2]

The commissioner's displeasure could not mask the fact that during the first 50 years of the Federal Trade Commission's existence, no substantive rules had been written except in a few in-

2 *Ibid.*, p. 190.

stances where they had been expressly authorized by laws such as the Fur Products Labeling Act of 1945. Whether the commissioners liked it or not, the opponents of the cigarette rule did have historical justification for expressing their doubt about the validity of the Federal Trade Commission's new procedure. Nonuse gave cigarette manufacturers some support for their argument that general rulemaking powers were not delegated by Congress.

Mr. Austern began his testimony before the commission by attempting to establish what the intent of Congress had been in creating the Federal Trade Commission in 1914. Discussing selected segments of floor debate that preceded the passage of the act and quoting Congressman F. C. Stevens of Minnesota, one of the five House members who managed the debate, Austern, focused on a passage in the debate that seemed to limit the legislative authority of the proposed commission.[3]

The trouble with relying on floor debate to establish congressional intent is that the clear language of the legislation itself and judicial interpretation of that language take precedence over what happened on the floor of Congress. Frequently, remarks that arise in debate are not well thought out. Furthermore, in a lengthy record of debate, one often uncovers statements that support contradictory positions.[4]

Many of the arguments developed in testimony by the Tobacco

---

[3] In the debate a colleague asked if the new agency would, in any sense, exercise legislative functions such as those exercised by the Interstate Commerce Commission. Mr. Stevens answered, "We desired clearly to exclude that authority from the power of the Commission." The Tobacco Institute pointed to this statement as evidence that the Federal Trade Commission was not meant to have rulemaking powers. See *Congressional Record,* 63rd 2nd p. 11084 (June 13, 1914).

[4] Senator Newlands, a sponsor of the Federal Trade Commission Act in the Senate, made it clear in the debate, for example, that he expected the commission to use discretionary rulemaking power. He argued that it would be up to the proposed Federal Trade Commission to affix meaning to the term "unfair competition." And he went on to indicate his reliance on the Interstate Commerce Commission as a model for the Federal Trade Commission. If the Interstate Commerce Commission could successfully determine rate structures and other regulatory matters through their rulemaking procedures, it could be assumed that the Federal Trade Commission could perform a similar function for the matters within its jurisdiction.

Institute had been anticipated by the commission. A lengthy document written by the Federal Trade Commission staff contained a detailed history of the smoking controversy, including 24 pages of careful argument supporting the FTC's defense of its rulemaking authority. The arguments set forth in this document were used to answer the tobacco interests' position at the hearings.

THE FEDERAL TRADE COMMISSION'S
DEFENSE OF ITS ACTION

The FTC defended its rulemaking procedures and authority through three separate, but closely related, arguments. One was that rulemaking authority had been delegated by Congress both implicitly and explicitly in the Act of 1914. The second argument drew on Supreme Court opinions that had encouraged administrative agencies to rely more heavily on rulemaking rather than adjudicatory procedures. And the third claimed that the commission was not really doing anything very new through its trade regulation rule procedure.

The commission, in support of its first argument, stated that Congress delegated to it the power to prevent unfair methods of competition and deceptive or unfair trade practices. This delegation is contained in section 5(a)(6) of the act: "the Commission is hereby empowered and directed to prevent persons, partnerships, or corporations . . . from using unfair methods of competition in commerce and unfair or deceptive acts or practices in commerce." The delegation of expressed powers to *prevent* those activities listed indicates that the Federal Trade Commission was to be more than a judicial agency acting in a remedial capacity through quasi-judicial procedures alone. Also, the act gives the commission extensive powers to investigate and inquire. These functions underscored the expectation that the commission was to take affirmative action by exercising rulemaking authority.

Another section of the Federal Trade Commission Act empowers the commission "to make rules and regulations for the purpose of carrying out the provisions of this Act." The Federal Trade Commission claimed that this section embraced the trade regulation rule procedure, even though the section was unnecessary because the basic mandate of the commission could not be fulfilled without rulemaking powers. The commissioners wrote, "It is implicit in the basic purpose and design of the Trade Commission Act as a whole, to establish an administrative agency for the prevention of unfair trade practices, that the commission should not be confined to quasi-judicial proceedings." [5]

The logic of the foregoing arguments involving the propriety of rulemaking as a device for carrying out the purposes of the act was the most persuasive element of the commission's defense of its action on the smoking issue. It was buttressed by the fact that the Supreme Court had accepted this logic numerous times in cases concerning the rulemaking authority of agencies. The Federal Trade Commission referred to a 1947 decision involving one of its sister agencies, the Securities and Exchange Commission. In that case the Court wrote, "the choice made between proceeding by a general rule or by individual, *ad hoc* litigation is one that lies primarily in the informed discretion of the administrative agency." [6]

The third of the commission's arguments in support of its new rulemaking procedure was not as persuasive as the others. It claimed that although the old trade practices rules, which came out of trade practice conferences, were usually advisory in nature, they did at times form the basis for formal enforcement proceedings. The "difference between trade practice and trade regulation rules is one of degree, not of kind." The commission argued further, "The trade regulation rule procedure is not a sudden innovation, but a natural outgrowth of the trade practices rule procedure. It is thus the culmination of more than 40 years of Commission rulemaking."

[5] *Trade Regulation Rule for the Prevention of Unfair or Deceptive Advertising and Labeling of Cigarettes in Relation to the Health Hazards of Smoking and Accompanying Statement of Basis and Purpose of Rule,* Federal Trade Commission document (n.d.), p. 141.

[6] *Securities and Exchange Commission v. Chenery Corporation,* 332 US 194, 203 (1947).

One response to this last argument is to ask, why adopt new procedures if the old ones are nearly the same or almost as good? The answer would have to be that there is a significant difference between what could be accomplished under the trade regulation rules and what could be done with the older, more informal, trade practices rules. The commission nearly refuted its own argument when, in a later section of its report, it explained how the new trade regulation rules could be used in adjudication:

> In . . . adjudicatory proceeding(s) the Commission could not use the trade practice rule to resolve any disputed issue of fact, or to dispense with the introduction of evidence required to make out a *prima facie* case. . . . However, in the case of a trade regulation rule, accompanied by and based upon determinations of fact made in accordance with statutory rulemaking procedures, the Commission could, in subsequent adjudicatory proceeding, rely not only on the propositions of law contained in the rule, but also on the underlying factual matters determined.[7]

In other words, the new rulemaking procedure was much more powerful than the old one. It was enforceable and could be used as the rule of law to be applied in subsequent agency adjudications; the informal trade practice rules were much more limited. The commission, in its explanation of how the new rules could be used in agency adjudicatory proceedings, was making the point the tobacco interests had already recognized; their understanding of this point accounts, in part, for their opposition to the Federal Trade Commission's proposal.

Although it is unusual for the commissioners of a regulatory agency or the head of an executive department to preside at rulemaking sessions, the FTC commissioners personally presided at the cigarette hearings. Ordinarily, someone on the staff of the commission or someone from the Division of Trade Regulation Rules sits

7 The above three quotes are from the Federal Trade Commission document, *Trade Regulations Rule for the Prevention of Unfair or Deceptive Advertising,* pp. 143, 144, and 246.

alone and hears testimony. After the record has been made, the commissioners examine it and decide whether or not to adopt the proposed rule. If they so desire, they can call a second set of hearings over which they may preside, either individually or as a group. They might also be persuaded by someone adversely affected by the rule to schedule more hearings, particularly if the commission finds that the first hearings left some questions unanswered.

ADMINISTRATIVE LAW JUDGES (HEARING EXAMINERS)

All of the regulatory commissions and several other agencies have assigned to them contingents of highly specialized individuals called administrative law judges.[8] There are over 780 of them in government, working in 22 agencies: [9]

1.	Department of Agriculture	5
2.	Atomic Energy Commission	1
3.	Civil Aeronautics Board	21
4.	Environmental Protection Agency	1
5.	Federal Communications Commission	15
6.	Federal Maritime Commission	7
7.	Federal Power Commission	15
8.	Federal Trade Commission	11

(cont.)

8 On August 19, 1972, an executive order eliminated the title "hearing examiner" and created the title "administrative law judge." (37 *Federal Register* 162, August 19, 1972.) The change had been sought for many years by the hearing examiners' association, the Federal Trial Examiners Conference (now called the Administrative Law Judges Conference).

9 These statistics were provided by the Office of Administrative Law Judges, United States Civil Service Commission. The growth in numbers of hearing examiners has been rapid. Between 1968 and 1974 the number increased from 600 to 780. This growth reflects the increase in rulemaking and adjudicatory powers exercised by agencies in recent years.

9. Interstate Commerce Commission 75
10. Department of Labor 10
11. Maritime Administration (Dept. of Commerce) 2
12. National Labor Relations Board 94
13. National Transportation Safety Board 6
14. Occupational Safety and Health Review Commission 41
15. Securities and Exchange Commission 7
16. U.S. Postal Service 2
17. U.S. Postal Rate Commission 1
18. U.S. Civil Service Commission 1
19. Department of Interior 26
20. U.S. Coast Guard (Dept. of Transportation) 16
21. Internal Revenue Service 1
22. Social Security Administration 420

Most of an administrative judge's time is devoted to adjudicatory proceedings, not rulemaking. In fact, the special, formal demands of adjudication were the chief reason for the creation of these interesting and unusual government positions. Nevertheless, one occasionally finds a judge presiding at rulemaking hearings. The administrative judges in the Department of Labor, for example, preside at hearings devoted to interpreting sections of the Fair Labor Standards Act.

The Federal Trade Commission's judges are not involved in rulemaking proceedings. Like other agencies, the FTC is reluctant to ask them to preside at these hearings because of the independence of these individuals from the agency to which they are assigned. This independence, both necessary and desirable in adjudication, is neither necessary nor desirable in rulemaking. Agencies like to have more control over policy development through rulemaking than the use of administrative law judges allows.

The administrative judges' status in the federal service is much different from that of all other agency personnel. They are, of course, employees of the government with civil service status and merit system protection. However, the nature of the judges' work requires that they be set apart from, and independent of, their agencies.

One student of the administrative process describes the apparent contradiction in an administrative judge's position as one that represents the tug of contrary traditions in our governmental system.[10] The tradition of an independent judiciary requires that disputes be settled according to well-established principles or laws by impartial judges. In their adjudicatory work, the judges are expected to uphold these traditions. At the same time, they are a part of the tradition of administrative efficiency and competency. In the administrative tradition, they are persons with expertise, working with others in the agency to develop and administer effective government programs. Important ingredients of the latter tradition are flexibility and adaptability to rapidly changing circumstances. The flexibility and technical competence required in regulatory, adjudicatory work conflict with the formalities of legal traditions at the point where the administrative judge enters the picture. The problem facing the government is to create and maintain a corps of individuals closely enough associated with the agency to assure that they are experts in the agency's complicated field, yet sufficiently detached to render impartial judgment in an adjudicatory proceeding.

The need for a cadre of judges or examiners arose shortly after creation of the Interstate Commerce Commission (ICC) in 1887. For nearly 20 years the commissioners of the Interstate Commerce Commission presided over all hearings. It became apparent during this period that the work load was too great and, further, that greater specialization and expertise were required for hearing and understanding the complexities of the cases before the commission.

Congress came to the aid of the Interstate Commerce Commission in 1906 when it authorized the commission to employ "separate agents or examiners." These individuals were hired to hear cases

---

10 Lloyd D. Musolf, *Federal Examiners and the Conflict of Law and Administration* (Baltimore: Johns Hopkins University Press, 1952), p. 173. For a series of recent studies on administrative law judges see *Administrative Law Review,* vol. 25, no. 1, Winter 1973. The entire issue is devoted to the subject.

and write an opinion before the commissioners were brought into the case. Their decisions were then passed on to the commission, where a final decision was made. The commissioners also reheard cases where they found an additional hearing was desirable or when an appeal from the examiner's decision was requested.

The appointment of hearing examiners in 1906 did help to relieve the burden on the ICC commissioners, but it also led to severe criticism of agency adjudication. As the number of hearing examiners grew, they became closely attached to their agencies and dependent upon them for salary increases and the like. They became less independent, making it difficult for them to maintain impartiality. Consequently, examiners bore the brunt of criticism from those who saw the traditional independence of the judiciary being eroded in agency adjudication presided over by individuals dependent upon the agency for their employment.

In 1941, the attorney general issued a report that required agencies to give more independence to hearing examiners. This report was also influential in persuading Congress to legislate eventually on the question of hearing examiners' separation from their agencies. The Administrative Procedure Act empowered the Civil Service Commission to supervise the corps of examiners. The Civil Service Commission, not the agency employing the examiner, was henceforth responsible for their hiring and rates of pay, removal, and discipline.[11]

To further insure the more detached, judicial demeanor of examiners or administrative law judges, the Administrative Procedure Act of 1946 requires that they behave according to some of the canons of judicial behavior. They cannot, for example, consult any party to the case outside of the hearings over which they preside, unless all parties participate in the consultation. Any *ex parte* communication such as telephone conversations or meetings in the corridors of the agency is frowned upon as unethical. Like their counterparts in the courts, administrative judges are expected to

11 Removal can occur only when "good cause" for such removal can be shown by the Civil Service Commission. Administrative judges, like other civil servants, are entitled to a hearing before removal is final.

refrain from discussing the case with anyone outside the hearing room. The act also requires that all communications with the judge during a hearing be made part of the public record. Furthermore, the judge is prohibited from participating in any of his agency's investigatory activities related to the development of a case he might hear. He first learns of a case and its details when the public hearing is scheduled.

The question of the independence of administrative judges was not completely resolved by Congress in the 1946 act. Shortly after it was passed, the judges' professional association sought and won a judgment in a district court that interpreted the Administrative Procedure Act in such a way as to increase the independence of examiners within the agencies to which they were assigned. The Federal Trial Examiners Conference (now the Administrative Law Judges Conference) wanted the court to rule that certain actions of the Civil Service Commission pertaining to promotion, compensation, and assignment of cases were invalid. They wanted to eliminate the variable pay classifications for examiners between agencies and the possibility of being dismissed in forced economy moves. The court agreed with the conference that Congress had intended administrative judges to be a special class of semi-independent officials within the agencies and that accession to these demands would help insure that independence. The government appealed to the Supreme Court and succeeded in having the lower court's decision reversed. The Supreme Court was not unanimous in its opinion, however. Three justices joined in a dissent favoring greater freedom for the judges in the interests of closer adherence to the judicial tradition:

> The Administrative Procedure Act was designed to give trial examiners . . . new status of freedom from agency control. Henceforth, they were to be "very nearly the equivalent of judges even though operating within the Federal system of administrative justice." [12]

[12] The dissenting justices expressed agreement with and quoted in their dissent this portion of the Senate floor debate on the Administrative Procedure

The 1953 Supreme Court decision did not diminish the prestige of the judges or seriously damage their independent status; they remain a select, prestigious group. The qualifications for appointment are quite rigorous. In addition to being a member of the bar, one must have had at least seven years of experience in preparation and presentation of cases in courts or before administrative agencies. A board of examiners within the Civil Service Commission evaluates the written materials and recommendations of applicants and administers oral examinations. Only about 10 percent of 4,000 eligible applicants have been appointed since 1964.[13]

The Federal Trade Commission has not used its judges in rulemaking even though they are now more readily available for this purpose due to a decrease in the amount of adjudicatory case work handled by the commission.[14] There is no legal barrier to assignment of administrative judges to preside over rulemaking hearings, but it appears unlikely that this will be done. When rules as controversial as cigarette labeling and advertising are being considered, the commissioners prefer to hear the testimony themselves. Other rulemaking hearings are so informal that it makes little sense to ask an administrative judge to preside since anyone familiar with the agency's activities and purposes can do it. But the principal reason for the commissioners' reluctance to ask judges to preside at rulemaking hearings is the semi-independent status that they enjoy. In legislative activities, the commissioners find it desirable to exercise more control over the course of the hearings than their limited authority over their contingent of judges would allow.

Act, *Ramspeck et al. v. Federal Trial Examiners Conference et al.,* 345 US 129 (1953).

[13] Charles J. Dullea, "Development of the Personnel Program for Administrative Law Judges," *Administrative Law Review,* vol. 25, no. 1, Winter 1973.

[14] The 1965 Annual Report of the commission noted that examiners were being used to perform some nonadjudicatory functions, but not rulemaking. Some had been lent to other agencies where the workload had increased.

PROMULGATION OF RULES

The official record remained "open" for two months after the Federal Trade Commission's cigarette hearings so those who desired to add additional statements to the official record could do so. After the record was closed, the commission issued its trade regulation rule on June 22, 1964. It was published in the *Federal Register* less than two weeks later. The commission also published a small announcement of the rule and a summary statement of its background and purpose, which was mailed to hundreds of people who had expressed some interest in this proceeding.

Publication of the trade regulation rule in the *Federal Register* marks the formal or official promulgation of the rule by the commission. Some months after it appears in the *Register,* it is published in cumulative volumes called the *Code of Federal Regulations.* All of the permanent rules and regulations made by administrative agencies are published in the *Code* and organized according to titles and subject matter. This repository of administrative law is similar in form to the volumes that contain the laws enacted by Congress, the *United States Code.*

Before 1948 there was no codification of the rules of administrative agencies that appeared in the *Federal Register.* The *Code of Federal Regulations,* which is the responsibility of the National Archives, has brought some order to the chaos that previously existed. Now it is possible for legal researchers to work systematically with administrative rules and regulations in much the same way they work with congressional enactments.

The rule that the commission adopted was nearly the same as the initial proposal, with one interesting exception. In the promulgated rule, the wording of the health warning was left up to the cigarette companies. (See the appendices for the text of the rule.) The warning language that was eventually written into the congressional legislation and now appears in all cigarette advertising was altered once and is the result of several years of negotiation between Congress, the FTC, and the manufacturers.

TOBACCO INTERESTS OBJECT TO THE RULE

The cigarette ruling was to have taken effect on January 1, 1965, about six months after the Federal Trade Commission published it in the *Register*.[15] In the period between the commission's hearings and the first of January, the cigarette interests mobilized in earnest. Within a month after the conclusion of the hearings, the industry announced the creation of a voluntary code.[16] This attempt at self-regulation was somewhat duplicative of the code administered by the National Association of Broadcasters (NAB), especially after the revision of the National Association of Broadcasters code during the summer of 1967. Duplication aside, creation of the voluntary code was intended to signify to Congress and the public that the industry was interested in regulating itself, and that the action of the Federal Trade Commission was an unnecessary obstacle to self-regulation.

Demonstrating their seriousness, the cigarette manufacturers hired former New Jersey Governor Robert B. Meyner to administer the code. He was empowered to fine violators up to $100,000. No one seems to know if any fines were levied against the member companies.[17] According to Governor Meyner, there were two major goals of the Cigarette Advertising Code: to prohibit advertising appeals to persons under 21 and to prohibit cigarette advertising health claims. Accordingly, cigarette advertisements were barred from certain publications with wide circulation among minors, for

15 The package warning label was required to appear on January 1, 1965 and the advertising warning six months later, July 1, 1965.

16 Nine major producers were signatories to the code: American Tobacco, R. J. Reynolds, Brown & Williamson, Larus and Brother, Liggett & Myers, P. Lorillard, Philip Morris, Stephano Brothers, and U.S. Tobacco. By 1968, code membership had dropped to six. For various reasons, P. Lorillard, American Tobacco, and Stephano Brothers quit the organization, which removed about one-third of total cigarette advertising revenues from code supervision.

17 See a comprehensive eight-part series on cigarette advertising by Louise Sweeney that appeared in the *Christian Science Monitor* during January and February, 1968.

c books and college newspapers. The code also at-
duce representations that connected smoking with
l conquests and acts that required physical stamina.
Any television program that had 45 percent or more of its viewers
under the age of 21 was off-limits for cigarette advertisers. The code
quietly went out of business six years later when cigarette advertising was banned from radio and television.

The code limitations on advertising were difficult to interpret
and enforce. These difficulties in part motivated an agreement that
led eventually to banning cigarette advertising from the broadcast
media. Programs obviously appealing to children, like *Captain
Kangaroo* and *Lassie*, did not tempt cigarette advertisers. Other
programs, which might have drawn young viewers, were more tempt-
ing. Senator Warren G. Magnuson, chairman of the Senate Commerce Committee, encouraged Governor Meyner to look more
closely at the sponsorship of television programs that appealed to
children. In a letter to Meyner, the senator reminded him, rather
bluntly, that a ban on all television advertising of cigarettes had
recently gone into effect in Great Britain. The Kent cigarette sponsorship of the Ed Sullivan show that included an appearance of
the Beatles had prompted the senator's letter. Later, sponsorship of
televised football games caused some dispute. Senator Robert F.
Kennedy joined Senator Magnuson in asking cigarette companies
to refrain from buying their $70,000-a-minute commercials from
CBS for the National Football League telecasts. The request, which
went to six cigarette producers, drew a mixed response, although
there was less cigarette advertising during the 1968 season. The
efficacy of the code in limiting the number of cigarette commercials
reaching people under 21 was questioned in a Federal Trade Commission report:

> The teenage exposure rate increased from 55.53 in January 1967 to
> 60.88 in January 1968 (a 9.6 percent jump) and the rate among chil-
> dren increased from 39.27 in January 1967 to 44.5 in January 1968
> (a 13.3 percent jump).[18]

[18] Federal Trade Commission, *Report to Congress*, June 30, 1968, p. 11
(mimeo.).

Congress reacted nearly as swiftly to the Federal Trade Commission's newly promulgated rule as the cigarette manufacturers did. After the announcement, members introduced 31 bills in the House and 4 in the Senate. All of the Senate bills were intended to support the FTC and strengthen government regulatory powers over cigarette producers. The House, which often responds more quickly to the pressures of special interests, found itself with 6 bills designed to strip the Federal Trade Commission of some of its powers to regulate cigarette advertising. The remaining 25 House bills were designed either to set up government research programs on smoking and health or to strengthen the Federal Trade Commission. The introduction of more bills favorable to the FTC's rule than opposed to it was not an indication of congressional support of the commission. Instead, congressional reaction was overwhelmingly negative, and it quickly became apparent from speeches on the floor and newspaper accounts that the Federal Trade Commission's action would not stand unchallenged. It is not unusual for bills to be introduced to reverse decisions of administrative agencies; however, most die without the formality of committee action. The cigarette interests had too much political muscle to allow the quiet death of the bills challenging the Federal Trade Commission. The first public indication of tobacco power in Congress came from Congressman Oren Harris (D.–Arkansas). Harris, then chairman of the House Interstate and Foreign Commerce Committee, requested that Chairman Dixon of the Federal Trade Commission delay implementation of the rule until the 89th Congress, which would convene in January 1965, had an opportunity to study it. Congress, according to Harris, feared prolonged litigation over the rule and thought that legislation was needed to clarify the situation. Harris's arguments were the same as those made by Mr. Austern at the commission hearings. Chairman Dixon yielded to congressional pressure and agreed to postpone the effective date of the Federal Trade Commission rule. Subsequently, congressional hearings were scheduled to begin in March in the Senate and April in the House.

The tobacco companies intended to make good on their threat to take the Federal Trade Commission to court if Congress failed to respond positively to their protestations against the advertising and labeling rule. The tobacco threat, voiced numerous times in the Federal Trade Commission hearings and in press releases, was hollow in the sense that the case against the commission was weak and most certainly would be decided by the courts in favor of the commission. The Federal Trade Commission knew that the tobacco case was weak, but they also knew that an appeal to the courts would take two or three years; this could have meant a postponement of the rule for at least that long. The postponement in itself would have been no small victory for the cigarette manufacturers.

JUDICIAL REVIEW OF ADMINISTRATIVE ACTIONS

Although delay might have been their primary motive, the cigarette manufacturers had the right to initiate a judicial proceeding to review the action of the Federal Trade Commission. Recourse to the courts is one of the protections provided an individual who believes that agency action interferes with his fundamental rights and liberties. The right to appeal an administrative decision to the courts is well established. The court is obliged to consider an appeal, but it can dismiss it quickly if the charge clearly is without merit. The extent to which a court will consent to fully substitute its judgment for that of an administrative agency is one of the most tangled areas in American jurisprudence. One of the reasons for this lack of clarity is that legal experience in administrative law is not as great as in other areas, which benefit from centuries of common law experience. And, in some respects, the functions of administrative agencies are outside the traditions of and incompatible with the common law. The common law did not anticipate the growth of administrative powers, and when these powers started to develop, they were met with a barrage of criticism from those who best understood and most vociferously defended the common law heritage.

One cannot fully understand the difficulties the courts face in developing a coherent approach to agency review and other agency matters unless he understands the resistance of common law to the development of agency adjudicatory and, to some extent, rulemaking powers. In 1885, a well-known British legal scholar, A. V. Dicey, wrote that in the common law system, no one could be lawfully punished or made to suffer in body or possessions except after due process before an ordinary court of law, that is, one in the regular independent judicial hierarchy. That being the case, the whole area of agency adjudication could be challenged on the grounds that it violated the fundamental precepts of an independent judiciary.[19] It took many years for the demands of the complex, modern state to break down the legal barriers in common law to agency action. As one might expect, that breakdown has been accompanied by much dispute and confusion.

The process of reconciling agency action with the common law is still going on. It is unclear and will be for some time on precisely what grounds agency actions can be overruled by the courts, and which actions, if any, are excluded from review. In some agency actions, statutes prohibit or limit court review. The Federal Trade Commission Act, for example, contains one of the common statutory limits on judicial review of administrative actions: "The findings of the Commission as to the facts, if supported by the evidence, shall be conclusive." This section of the act indicates one area of law where agencies and the courts have come to some agreement on the subject of review, at least at a high level of generalization. The courts have developed what is sometimes called the law-fact dichotomy, although in practice it is difficult to distinguish between the two. Generally the courts concern themselves with questions of law, while questions of fact are left to the agencies. The courts are most interested in seeing that agency *procedures* do not infringe upon an individual's fundamental rights and that agency decisions are based upon a proper understanding of relevant statutes and judicial precedents. At the same time, the courts recognize that agencies are better qualified than they are to consider and determine the facts of a case.

[19] A. V. Dicey, *Introduction to the Study of the Law of the Constitution* (London: Macmillan, 1885).

How does this division work out in practice? Suppose an agency had failed to grant a company a license to operate a television station. If the company appealed the agency decision to the courts on the grounds that the agency failed to properly recognize its capabilities for such an undertaking, the courts would probably dismiss the appeal without fully reconsidering the agency decision. The courts would say that the ability of one applicant to operate a television station as opposed to another is a question of fact, and the agency is better equipped to make those determinations than are the courts. In exercising this type of self-restraint, the courts are simply acknowledging the reason for the creation of the agency in the first place, i.e., to make policy determinations where the courts lack the necessary expertise.

There are many gray areas surrounding the law-fact dichotomy, partly because the separation of law from fact is usually quite difficult. Furthermore, there are some circumstances when the court will fully rehear cases when only the facts are at dispute. Although the courts are reluctant to put themselves in the agency's shoes on questions of fact, a court might do so when a party to a dispute complains that the agency decision was not supported by the evidence presented to the agency. This accusation implies that there might have been something awry with the procedures the agency used in hearing the case. And the courts have reserved for themselves the task of reviewing agency decisions when it appears that the procedures used by the agency were unfair.

In disputes of law concerning agency procedures, the courts seek to determine if the agency has acted fairly, without caprice, and in a manner that is not arbitrary. The court will explore these fundamental legal questions, and if it determines that the agency has violated the rights of an individual, it has the power to remand the case to the agency for another hearing or to dismiss the agency decision entirely. This holds true even when a statute might prohibit review. In a sense, all agency action is reviewable if the agency does not exercise its power properly. A part of the Administrative Procedure Act details some of the fundamental violations that could lead to review:

. . . the reviewing court shall decide all relevant questions of law, interpret constitutional and statutory provisions, and determine the meaning or applicability of the terms of any agency action. . . . It shall (A) compel agency action unlawfully withheld or unreasonably delayed; and (B) hold unlawful and set aside agency action . . . found to be (1) arbitrary, capricious, an abuse of discretion, or otherwise not in accordance with law; (2) contrary to constitutional right, power, privilege, or immunity; (3) in excess of statutory jurisdiction, authority, or limitations, or short of statutory right; (4) without observance of procedure required by law. . . .

As long as the agency's procedures are fair and the decision is based upon a correct understanding of the governing legal standards, courts are reluctant to interfere. The courts have accepted the expertise of the agencies in dealing with questions of fact and, in most cases involving such questions, dismiss appeals from agency decisions.

Adjudicatory proceedings of agencies are subject to closer judicial scrutiny than rulemaking. Because the procedural requirements for agency adjudication are similar to judicial procedures while agency rulemaking procedures can be as lax as those of congressional committees, there are far fewer grounds upon which an agency rule might be appealed to the courts. Outside of flagrant and obvious impairment of fundamental rights, another substantial problem is whether the rule promulgated by the agency is rationally related to the purposes of the statute the rule is intended to implement.

When the cigarette companies were faced with the prospect of filing an appeal, they realized they would have to claim that the Federal Trade Commission had exceeded its powers in issuing the rule. They had to argue that Congress had not delegated these powers to the commission, but in the light of the Supreme Court's previous reactions to such arguments, the cigarette case looked very weak indeed.

If the cigarette companies had decided to take an appeal, it would have been filed with a United States Court of Appeals, since all appeals from agency decisions, with the exception of those from the Interstate Commerce Commission, go to this middle tier of the federal judicial system.[20] If they had received an unfavorable decision in a court of appeals, they could have filed for a *writ of certiorari* in the Supreme Court. If the high Court grants review, the final action is taken at that level; if not, the decision of the court of appeals stands.

While an appeal to the courts was being considered, lines in Congress were being drawn for the cigarette battle. The cigarette manufacturers had in the past been able to rely on Congress to kill any serious attempt by government agencies to interfere with their business. Now circumstances were different. The antismoking forces had the Surgeon General's report and a ruling by the Federal Trade Commission to bolster their position. Furthermore, a rather impressive number of senators and representatives had begun to associate themselves with the commission's action. A prelude to the difficulties that the tobacco interests were to face had arisen unexpectedly shortly before the FTC hearings in the spring of 1964. An amendment was attached to a crop support bill in the Senate that would have abolished the tobacco support and acreage control programs. It was defeated, handily, by a vote of 63 to 26, but this frontal assault shook the tobacco men, and the amendment took them by surprise. This was the first floor test of cigarette sentiment since the Surgeon General's report. It showed the tobacco lobbyists that they would have to work diligently to keep the sympathy they were accustomed to finding in Congress. To that end, the industry mobilized a very impressive lobbying team, a team that was at work well before the 89th Congress convened in January, 1965.

[20] The courts of appeals were created in 1891, three years after the creation of the Interstate Commerce Commission. This historical situation accounts for the exception in ICC appeals procedure.

7

CONGRESSIONAL POWER
AND AGENCY POLICYMAKING

When he was Senate minority leader, Everett McKinley Dirksen spoke lyrically of the exalted place of Congress in the governmental system at a meeting of the American Political Science Association. In his engaging manner, he directed the thoughts of his audience to Article One, Section Eight of the Constitution, which says, "Congress shall have the *power*. . . ." Looking heavenward, the senator said wistfully, "I *love* those words."

Among the implications of the senator's comment is the suggestion that Congress has the strength to control the powers it delegates to administrative agencies. Although this view might accord with the formal constitutional distribution of powers, it inaccurately describes the realities of contemporary politics. Congressmen might dream of a parliamentary Camelot where they control, direct, or perhaps substantially influence all of the actions of the 2.6 million civilians who work in the bureaucracy, but the hard facts of the modern policy process often shatter that dream.

CONGRESSIONAL OVERSIGHT

Article One, Section Eight has not been repealed, and Congress does have the power to oversee the activities of administrative agencies. These agencies exist because Congress created them; they make policy because Congress delegates the authority for them to do so and appropriates funds for their continuing operation. Yet Congress has considerable difficulty controlling, in meaningful, constructive ways, the agencies it creates. Just as parents have some difficulty controlling their children, Congress often finds its administrative offspring uncontrollable. Congress can harass, it can block temporarily, but its long-term influence is questionable. As in the parent-child relationship, the causes of family or governmental conflicts are found in the characteristics and attitudes of the parent, Congress, the children, agencies, and society at large. Agencies are more nimble and persistent than their cumbersome congressional parent. And they have the advantage of expertise derived from the ability to concentrate on a limited group of related issues until they understand the issues and their ramifications better than anyone else.

The complex problems of modern society also tend to strengthen agencies in their relations with Congress. In foreign affairs, for example, Congress has been virtually removed from meaningful policy participation; leadership resides increasingly and securely in the executive and its agencies. A similar situation exists in the domestic sphere. Congress as an institution has more in its purview than the activities of any single agency. Even if it could become more specialized to compete with bureaucratic expertise, it would be hard pressed to find time to keep up with the voluminous productivity of the agencies. So Congress, or its component parts, has to choose the issues it wants to concentrate upon and carefully prepare itself to question the agencies on these issues. A great deal of congressional time and thought goes into making decisions regarding which policies are to be scrutinized.

Congressional oversight of agency operations in nearly all cases is the responsibility of the committees or subcommittees within an agency's policy subsystem. Formal oversight can occur in annual appropriation hearings, hearings on proposed legislation, or occasional investigations.[1] The quality of oversight varies from subsystem to subsystem; some agencies are subjected to detailed scrutiny of expenditures down to the number of new typewriters ordered; others receive more general and enlightened policy guidance. The fact that subcommittees are generally responsible for oversight means that from the agency's point of view a few congressmen are more important than Congress as a whole. All agencies, then, operate with the knowledge that their overseeing committees and, particularly, the leaders of these committees can wreak havoc upon their programs. This knowledge frequently leads to overcautious agency administration that is more concerned about responding to the wishes of a few members of Congress than to what might be the general, though unarticulated, desire of Congress or the nation as a whole.

Overdependence on small numbers of important congressmen can lead to unethical and even illegal interference in agency matters by powerful members of Congress on behalf of a constituent. Individual member intervention in agency affairs or informal oversight could be quite innocent in appearance. Yet even an innocent congressional query could have unsavory overtones. What if a member queries the chairman of a regulatory commission about progress in awarding a certain license? This might be a perfectly innocuous question, but it could lead to an unfair advantage for that congressman's constituent in a situation where there was competition for

---

[1] See Joseph P. Harris, *Congressional Control of Administration* (Washington, D.C.: The Brookings Institution, 1964) for a description of the formal oversight functions of Congress.

that license.[2] In short, it is difficult to generalize about the nature, quality, and ethics of congressional oversight. One suspects that it is weak both in terms of general policy guidance and influence on the millions of policy decisions that bureaucrats make. On the other hand, it can be devastating to an agency that out of ignorance or bravery defies the wishes of its small, but powerful and important congressional constituency.

THE FEDERAL TRADE COMMISSION'S
OVERSIGHT STRUGGLE

In view of most congressional oversight, the actions of Congress against the Federal Trade Commission's attempts to require health warnings for cigarette smokers were unusual both in their form and severity. Congress passed a bill in 1965 that reduced in very specific terms a small portion of the FTC's powers. Oversight legislation of a punitive nature is frequently introduced by an irate member, but it seldom is passed or even given serious committee consideration. Normally, reprimands of agencies are informal, handled by committees through threatened action or by an actual reduction of an agency's budget. Either of these occurrences may take place without introduction of legislation or without public hearings.

Open controversy between Congress and an agency is almost always avoided, an indication that those within a subsystem know each other's attitudes and positions fairly well before an agency tries something new. But in the mid-1960s, the pressure exerted on the Federal Trade Commission by the health interests and the Surgeon General's report encouraged the commission to take an action

[2] The history of the regulatory commissions has been haunted by frequent investigations of unfair or unethical interference by members of Congress, and the general public, in the decision-making process. Some investigations, like the one into the Sherman Adams affair, have reached into government's highest places. For a discussion of these problems see Emmette S. Redford, *American Government and the Economy* (New York: Macmillan, 1965), especially chapter 25, and Bernard Schwartz, *The Professor and the Commissions* (New York: Alfred A. Knopf, 1959).

that was to invoke the full wrath of Congress. The threat of a warning being required on cigarette packages and in all advertising was more than Congress was prepared to accept. It appeared that no one in the FTC had bothered to check its proposed cigarette rule in advance with the appropriate members of Congress. Perhaps the rule had not been cleared with the Hill because of the newness of the rulemaking procedure and the commission's inexperience with it.

The resulting congressional reprimand of the Federal Trade Commission was unexpectedly severe in its intensity. It involved lengthy hearings in both houses of Congress on the substance and wisdom of the FTC action. The legislation that emerged from those hearings specifically negated the commission's rule and temporarily took away its rulemaking powers relating to cigarette advertising.[3] The commission was prohibited from requiring or even considering the requirement of a health warning in cigarette advertising for four years. The jurisdiction of the commission under the 1914 act was not changed; its new, controversial trade regulation rule procedure was left intact except as it applied to cigarette regulation. The pinpoint accuracy of the congressional oversight was so unusual that old-timers on Capitol Hill could not remember when or if it had ever happened that way before.

To compound this significant departure from the traditional politics of oversight, a similar, but in some ways more bizarre, provision was included in the cigarette legislation passed in 1970. In this act, Congress changed the wording of the health warning and continued some of the provisions of the 1965 act. One of the provisions it extended was the prohibition against FTC action—this time for a period of two years. There was a new twist, however. The FTC was required to give Congress six months' notice of any plans it might have thereafter to adopt a trade regulation rule affecting cigarettes. Along with the notice of such contemplated action, the commission was required to submit supporting evidence for its proposed rule. The purpose of the six months' notice, stated

[3] PL 89–92 (1965), U.S.C., sect. 1331.

explicitly in the legislation, was to give Congress the time to act if it should desire to do so.[4] Never again would Congress be confronted by FTC cigarette rulemaking without adequate warning.

The pinpointing by Congress of a specific action and the commission's inability to muster support for what it had done left the Federal Trade Commission a bit shaken. The effectiveness of those acts of congressional oversight should not be interpreted to mean that Congress can effectively exercise a veto over all agency actions. There is insufficient time in the course of a congressional session to handle most such matters. Yet the fact that Congress has the power to rise up in awesome dissent, at least occasionally, serves to remind administrators that the road to success is paved with quietly negotiated accommodation of agency policy to the views of key congressmen. In this way Congress exercises rather firm control over agency activities.

NO VICTORY FOR HEALTH

Congress was not acting alone when it moved against the Federal Trade Commission. It was assisted by the skills, rhetorical and organizational, of the Tobacco Institute and the allies recruited by the institute. The lobbying effort mounted by this group was brilliantly conceived; it indicated that the cigarette manufacturers had the good sense to adapt their approach to the changing tides of public demand in the health field. The manufacturers saw the beginning of a breakdown in the tobacco subsystem, and they had the political acumen and sensibility to shift their tactics to cope with it. They turned what could have been a substantial threat to the steady expansion of cigarette sales into a limited victory. The Cigarette Labeling and Advertising Act passed by Congress in 1965 was more of a victory for cigarettes than it was for health.

The cigarette manufacturers realized that public demands for action in response to the research on smoking and health were

4 PL 91–222 (1970), 15 U.S.C., sect. 1331.

much stronger than they had been in the past. The health forces had been strengthened by the Surgeon General's 1964 report, *Smoking and Health*. And it was becoming increasingly clear that the cigarette manufacturers would no longer be able to bury or ignore the criticisms of the health people as they had in the past. The industry's attempts to find a safer cigarette and to mitigate the adverse findings of health research by counter, pro-cigarette research had resulted in very little data favorable to smoking. Consequently, promises for even more research, voluntary advertising codes, and a less dangerous cigarette could no longer be used to stay the momentum that the antismoking people had been able to build. Armed with the Federal Trade Commission rule, the Surgeon General's report, and some public support, the health groups had many things going for them in 1965. The carefully constructed walls of tobacco defense were beginning to crack.

The political assets of the health people in Washington were enhanced by the successes some of their colleagues were having with state and local governments. Cigarette package warnings had been proposed for New York City by the city health commissioner. Similar suggestions were being considered by New York, Massachusetts, and other states. The governor of California had created a cigarette smoking advisory committee, and in several jurisdictions pressure was growing to enforce laws already on the books that banned cigarette sales to minors. Indeed, one month before President Johnson signed the Cigarette Labeling and Advertising Act (on July 27, 1965), Governor Nelson A. Rockefeller of New York signed into law a requirement that all cigarette packages sold in his state carry a health warning. If there was anything the cigarette companies wanted less than federal regulation, it was state requirements that health warnings appear. This could have meant as many different labels as there are states, creating an obvious marketing problem.

In the face of mounting concern over cigarette smoking as a health hazard, there was genius in the Cigarette Labeling and Advertising bill from the industry point of view. The bill contained just enough regulation to pass as a health measure; and while the bill required a health warning, it also contained provisions to dismantle an important part of the work of the Federal Trade Commission. Its most significant provision in these terms was the section that temporarily eliminated the FTC's rulemaking power in the cigarette advertising field.

The bill as originally introduced permanently banned such Federal Trade Commission action. When the bill was passed, Congress had reduced the length of the ban to four years or until July 1, 1969. Another important provision of the bill prohibited other federal agencies, for example, the Federal Communications Commission, from taking any action to require health warnings in advertising. State and local action was also blocked or preempted by congressional action. Foreclosing the possibility of state and local regulation was a major attraction of the bill for the cigarette manufacturers.

Despite the inclusion of these provisions, the bill was written in terms of protecting public health. The text of the act begins by declaring that it was the intention of Congress to establish a federal program to inform the public of the possible health hazards of smoking. To this end Congress appropriated $2 million shortly after the labeling act was passed, to establish the National Clearinghouse for Smoking and Health. This agency, which is part of the Public Health Service, carries out educational campaigns and collects data on smoking and health research in the United States. In a sense, this was the only significant provision of the bill for the health interests. The package labeling requirement was thought by most to be rather insignificant as long as no warning had to appear in advertising. As the controversy over the bill developed in Congress, it became clear that the tobacco interests thought they had little to fear from the labeling requirement.

As the final votes neared, there was virtually no opposition to the bill from the cigarette manufacturers. On the contrary, they seemed to be supporting it. The bill passed the Senate by a vote of 72 to 5, with most of the tobacco state senators voting for it. Senators who argued that what was being sold as a public health measure was little more than a boon to the cigarette interests voted against it.[5] Even those who often raised objections to bills that granted the national government regulatory powers instead of allowing the states to have them were quiet on the labeling bill. There were no recorded southern or conservative objections to that part of the bill that prohibited the states from adopting similar or related regulatory legislation.

The House adopted the bill by voice vote under circumstances that were designed to limit debate and dissension. The bill was brought to the floor and passed on a Tuesday afternoon when there were only a few members present. The chief opponent of the bill, John Moss (D.–California), had been informed earlier that the vote would come on the following Thursday. When the vote was taken, he was in a commercial aircraft over the Atlantic flying back from Europe. This switch in scheduling violated the gentlemen's agreement that governs such matters in Congress. Congressman Richard Bolling (D.–Missouri) spoke of the questionable tactics of bringing the labeling bill to the floor early:

". . . the Committee [Interstate and Foreign Commerce] was able to get through this House of Representatives a piece of legislation which it agreed upon, when the only person who opposed the legislation strongly enough to sign a minority report was known to be away and unable to return. . . ." [6]

The committee chairman, Mr. Harris, denied having any knowledge that his dissenting committee member was out of the country. This episode and other earlier signs discouraged Moss and his liberal colleagues from protesting loudly or fighting with any enthusiasm against the labeling bill in the House. The liberal Democratic Study Group, sensing the overwhelming support for the

[5] Four of the opposition votes were cast by liberal Democrats: Paul Douglas of Illinois, Robert Kennedy of New York, Gaylord Nelson of Wisconsin, and Joseph Clark of Pennsylvania. The fifth was from a Republican, Senator Wallace Bennett of Utah, a Mormon and longtime foe of cigarette smoking.

[6] *Congressional Record*, p. H15962, July 13, 1965.

cigarette manufacturers, decided against organizing any opposition to the bill.[7]

The House was considerably more pro-cigarette than the Senate. Realization of this factor by all parties shifted the scene of the most intense activity to the Senate, and especially the Senate Commerce Committee. The Senate could be expected to go along with that committe's very powerful and popular chairman, Warren Magnuson (D.–Washington). The strength of the tobacco interests in the House, as opposed to the Senate, could be seen in the conference that followed the passage of the bill in each chamber. The House had passed a permanent ban on the Federal Trade Commission's involvement in cigarette advertising; the Senate conferees forced their House counterparts to accept a maximum four-year limit. In the bargaining, the House refused to accept the Senate provision that the printed warning appear on the front of cigarette packages; instead, the conferees agreed to leave the decision concerning where the warning would appear up to the manufacturers.

The passage of the Cigarette Labeling and Advertising Act was a major victory for cigarette manufacturers and their allies. The unwary might find that interpretation difficult to accept; yet this interpretation can be supported. Cigarette manufacturers needed some legislation from Congress, or the much more onerous Federal Trade Commission rule would stand. The ruling could have been challenged in the courts, but the success of any such challenge was questionable. The courts today are inclined to accept the rulemaking actions of administrative agencies as long as proper procedures are used in formulating the rule. Consequently, the

---

[7] Organized in 1956, the Democratic Study Group (DSG) consists of House Democratic liberals who oppose the dominant conservative leadership in the House. The group first indicated its strength and principles when called upon to oppose the Southern Manifesto of 1956, a document sponsored by nearly all Southern Democrats, which opposed civil rights measures. The DSG proved effective in winning some liberal reforms in the early 1960s. For more on the DSG, see Richard Bolling, *House Out of Order* (New York: E. P. Dutton, 1965), pp. 54–58, and Mark F. Ferber, "The Formation of the Democratic Study Group," in Nelson W. Polsby (Ed.), *Congressional Behavior* (New York: Random House, 1971).

tobacco manufacturers' best strategy was to support legislation that could be passed in Congress and which would not retard cigarette sales. One observer commented upon the cigarette triumph in these terms: "In fact . . . the bill is not, as its sponsors suggested, an example of congressional initiative to protect public health; it is an unashamed act to protect private industry from government regulation." [8]

STRATEGY FOR SUCCESS

How did the cigarette manufacturers manage to win such an impressive victory? What led to their success in persuading Congress to do what the Federal Trade Commission could not be persuaded to do? These enviable accomplishments were designed and executed under the very able leadership of former Senator Earle C. Clements of Kentucky.

Senator Clements's experience on the Hill provided him with both the knowledge of congressional operations and the personal support from members he needed to be effective. His one-time executive directorship of the Senate Democratic Campaign Fund enabled him to draw on the assets of old political favors. Aside from his power in Congress, the former senator was one of the few men who could keep President Johnson out of the controversy. Mr. Johnson had as good, if not better, a record on consumer legislation than any president in memory. Yet he made no public attempt to support the Federal Trade Commission in its struggle on the Hill. He was uncharacteristically silent during the whole affair, from the announcement of the congressional hearings through the bill-signing formality.

Senator Clements was hired by the six largest cigarette manufacturers in 1964. Reinforcing the strategy to downgrade the Federal Trade Commission's rulemaking authority, Clements was at work

[8] Elizabeth Brenner Drew, "The Quiet Victory of the Cigarette Lobby: How It Found the Best Filter Yet—Congress," *The Atlantic Monthly*, September, 1965, p. 76.

in Congress well before the commission had even adopted its rule. The first thing he had to do was coordinate the thinking and strategies of the cigarette manufacturers and their allies. He knew that success could very well depend on how quickly and firmly he could forge a united front among the manufacturers, tobacco state congressmen, growers, advertisers, and other friends of the cigarette business.

Clements rightly sensed that this time the cigarette companies were going to be forced to give up something; the protestations of the health groups were too strong to be ignored. He decided to persuade his employers to accept the label on packages in return for a ban against a similar requirement in advertising and a ban against state action requiring health warnings. This strategy, which seems so sensible in light of its success, did not seem as sensible when the former senator began his work.

Shortly after Senator Clements arrived in Washington, he scheduled regular weekly meetings with the Tobacco Institute's attorneys, public relations firms, and friends. The public relations firm of Hill and Knowlton had been on retainer to the institute since its inception. While not registered as lobbyists, Hill and Knowlton represented the Washington interests of firms estimated to account for more than ten percent of the gross national product.[9] At these meetings detailed plans were worked out for the Federal Trade Commission hearings, for congressional lobbying, and for a possible appeal to the courts should all else fail. Once it was decided that Congress should be the prime target, it was obvious that the Senate Commerce Committee held the key to victory.

Senator Clements knew that both houses could be expected to

---

[9] It is difficult to be certain about how much is spent on the institute's lobbying campaigns in any one year. The industry spends about $300 million annually on promotion, advertising, and public relations. A small clue to the portion of this that is directed toward lobbying the general public and Congress against anticigarette legislation was contained in a news story in the *Christian Science Monitor*. According to that newspaper, the Tobacco Institute signed a $437,000 contract with the Tiderock Corporation of New York City for legislative purposes in October, 1967. (Reported by Louise Sweeney, "Tobacco Institute Defends Advertising," *Christian Science Monitor*, February 6, 1968.)

follow the dictates of their committees. Generally, the whole body affirms the work of its committees; moreover, floor revolts are even less likely than usual against the commerce committees because of their important jurisdictions. Members are not anxious to jeopardize a favorable relationship with these committees by failing to heed their recommendations.

The Interstate and Foreign Commerce Committee is a rather conservative force in the House, and Southerners held key positions in 1965.[10] The chairman, Oren Harris, represented a rural area in Arkansas, and the second ranking member, Harley Staggers, was from a similar area of West Virginia. Seven other members of the 33-man committee were from tobacco regions, including Congressman Horace R. Kornegay of North Carolina, who was a vociferous advocate for the tobacco companies. Kornegay decided not to run for Congress in 1968. Instead he assumed the post of vice-president and counsel of the Tobacco Institute in January, 1969.

[10] Membership of the House Interstate and Foreign Commerce Committee in 1965:

Democrats	Republicans
Oren Harris, chairman (Arkansas)	William Springer (Illinois)
Harley Staggers (West Virginia)	J. Arthur Younger (California)
Walter Rogers (Texas)	Samuel L. Devine (Ohio)
Samuel Friedel (Maryland)	Ancher Nelson (Minnesota)
Torbert Macdonald (Massachusetts)	Hastings Keith (Massachusetts)
John Jarman (Oklahoma)	Willard Curtin (Pennsylvania)
Lee O'Brien (New York)	Glenn Cunningham (Nebraska)
John Moss (California)	James T. Broyhill (North Carolina)
John Dingell (Michigan)	James Harvey (Michigan)
Paul Rogers (Florida)	Tim Lee Carter (Kentucky)
Horace Kornegay (North Carolina)	Howard H. Callaway (Georgia)
Lionel Van Deerlin (California)	
J. J. Pickle (Texas)	
Fred Rooney (Pennsylvania)	
John M. Murphy (New York)	
David Satterfield (Virginia)	
Daniel J. Ronan (Illinois)	
J. Oliva Huot (New Hampshire)	
James A. Mackay (Georgia)	
John Gilligan (Ohio)	
Charles P. Farnsley (Kentucky)	
John Bell Williams (Mississippi)	

The Senate Commerce Committee was more consumer oriented than its House counterpart. It was beginning to develop and report out bills on a series of consumer matters unrelated to cigarettes except for their common purposes of strengthening protection of the public from business abuses. The membership of the committee was closely divided over the cigarette issue, making the chairman, Senator Magnuson, of crucial importance to both the smoking and the health forces.[11] He was careful to avoid committing himself to either group at an early date.

Senator Neuberger worked strenuously to rally support for the health forces among her colleagues on the committee. Her work was destined to be unproductive because she faced a united Republican opposition under the leadership of Thruston Morton, the popular senator from Kentucky. Senators Vance Hartke of Indiana and Ross Bass of Tennessee, both Democrats, were unsympathetic to the pleas of their colleague. Senator Bass had a sizeable tobacco constituency, and Senator Hartke was indebted to Earle Clements for his aid as director of the Senate Democratic Campaign Fund. Hartke was subject to no strong pressures from his constituency on either side of the smoking issue, so he displayed some loyalty to those who had been loyal to him. The six Republicans and two Democrats united in opposition to the senator from Oregon, plus some wavering Democrats unenthusiastic about the health position,

[11] Membership of the Senate Commerce Committee in 1965:

Democrats	*Republicans*
Warren G. Magnuson, chairman (Washington)	Norris Cotton (New Hampshire)
John O. Pastore (Rhode Island)	Thruston Morton (Kentucky)
A. S. "Mike" Monroney (Oklahoma)	Hugh Scott (Pennsylvania)
Frank Lausche (Ohio)	Winston Prouty (Vermont)
E. L. Bartlett (Alaska)	James B. Pearson (Kansas)
Vance Hartke (Indiana)	Peter Dominick (Colorado)
Gale W. McGee (Wyoming)	
Philip A. Hart (Michigan)	
Howard W. Cannon (Nevada)	
Daniel Brewster (Maryland)	
Maurine Neuberger (Oregon)	
Ross Bass (Tennessee)	

made Mrs. Neuberger's attempt to give congressional approval to the Federal Trade Commission ruling impossible. It became clear as the hearings began that the Federal Trade Commission action would be either reversed or substantially modified in the Senate Commerce Committee. The health groups could not rally the necessary political support to prevent Congress from changing the FTC's rule.

The antismoking forces were not nearly as well organized or as well financed as the cigarette interests. Lobbyist David Cohen of the Americans for Democratic Action characterized the contest between the tobacco people and the health people as similar to a match between the Green Bay Packers and a high school football team. The tobacco state congressmen had powerful reasons to reverse the Federal Trade Commission action, namely, their constituents' support. On the other hand, there were few if any "health" congressmen. Those members who did champion the health cause had no substantial constituent interest to back them up.

In the absence of support from special interest constituencies, congressmen find it difficult to vote for regulatory measures that are unpopular across the whole business and industrial spectrum. Consequently, they find it relatively easy to vote funds for health research but difficult to vote for programs that would end or reduce those hazards that are identified in the health research they sponsored, as indicated in this statement:

> The lawmakers enthusiastically vote hundreds of millions of dollars— more, usually, than is requested—for health research, for when it is simply a matter of research, what congressman is against health? However, when the officials go to Capitol Hill with proposals to put research findings into effect—to curb air pollution or discourage smoking—they are skunks at the lawn party. For on these issues there are large economic issues at stake.[12]

12 Drew, *op. cit.,* p. 79.

THE HEALTH LOBBY

The efforts of health organizations outside of Congress were no more successful than they were inside. Those who might have benefited from the cigarette legislation were confirmed or prospective smokers, and neither group was particularly interested in creating any government program geared to pointing out the group's foolishness. The public health interest groups have very small constituencies, usually coalitions of the various professionals in fields related to medicine and health. These people find it difficult to devote the time and resources necessary to put their complex, technical reasoning before the public and convince them of its validity. Instead, their activities are confined primarily to research and fund raising. Consequently, these groups, the American Cancer Society, the American Heart Association, the National Tuberculosis Association, and others, confined most of their activities to the hearing rooms.[13]

The health and consumer oriented agencies in government were weak in the face of organized congressional opposition. The Federal Trade Commission, for example, had little clout with committees on the Hill because it had virtually no support from its constituents, the industries it regulated. Without good congressional connections or an active clientele group, the commission was in a poor position to do battle with Congress.[14] Paul Rand Dixon, chair-

[13] The American Medical Association (AMA) did not testify in Congress although it took the position publicly that Congress, not the Federal Trade Commission, should regulate the cigarette industry, if there had to be any regulation at all. This position drew criticism from the more liberal members of the organization. They wanted the AMA to speak out on this health problem. On June 24, 1965, the American Medical Association did adopt a resolution noting a significant relationship between cigarette smoking and the incidence of lung cancer. However, the resolution was adopted after both Senate and House had already passed the labeling bill. The AMA had received $10 million in research grants from six tobacco companies a few weeks after the Federal Trade Commission's hearings a year before, in the spring of 1964.

[14] See Norton E. Long, "Power and Administration," *Public Administration Review*, Volume 9, Autumn, 1949, pp. 257–264.

man of the FTC, had little desire to stir more controversy in Congress than he had done already with the adoption of the rule. He testified on behalf of the commission, but there is little evidence of any meaningful activity on his part outside of the hearing room.

The Public Health Service was similarly ill equipped to lead a legislative struggle to protect the sanctity of its *Smoking and Health* report. The Public Health Service has a large annual budget it likes to preserve; furthermore, it never demonstrated much competence in lobbying for substantive legislation. Its parent organization, the Department of Health, Education and Welfare, had declared at an earlier date that it would not wholeheartedly support the action of the Federal Trade Commission.

The health groups acted as if they knew there was little hope for legislation supporting the ruling of the Federal Trade Commission. They too sensed the opposition in the House and devoted very little time to attempting to overcome what was insurmountable opposition. Instead, they devoted most of their time to the Senate, but given the House opposition, they knew their efforts in the upper chamber held little promise of bringing a strong piece of legislation out of Congress.

The health groups made some concerted attempts to take their case directly to the public. To facilitate their campaign, they formed an organization called the National Interagency Council on Smoking and Health in July 1964. The council had 16 charter members and currently has 34 members plus five affiliated organizations.[15]

[15] The following groups are members of the council: American Academy of Pediatrics, American Association of Health, Physical Education, and Recreation, American Cancer Society, American College of Chest Physicians, American College Health Association, American College of Physicians, American College of Radiology, American College of Surgeons, American Dental Association, American Heart Association, American Hospital Association, American Medical Association, American Nurses Association, American Pharmaceutical Association, American Public Health Association, American School Health Association, Association of Classroom Teachers of the NEA, Association of State and Territorial Health Officers, Boys' Clubs of America, National Board of Young Men's Christian Association, National Board of Young Women's Christian Association, National Congress of Parents and Teachers, National Jogging Association, National

The chairman of the council during the labeling hearings was Emerson Foote, described by the Tobacco Institute as a "one-time advertising man, and 'reformed' smoker, who made a small fortune peddling cigarettes." [16] The characterization did not do justice to the unusual career of this man. Emerson Foote came to Madison Avenue in 1936 and began one of the advertising industry's most successful promotional schemes. He handled the Lucky Strike account and wrote most of the slogans that not only made his client prosperous but also popularized smoking throughout the nation. When he decided to join the health forces, he was chairman of the board of McCann-Erickson, one of the country's largest advertising firms. Foote explained that his decision to switch rather than fight for the cigarette manufacturers did not grow out of a dislike for cigarettes: "I am not against tobacco. I am against cancer, heart disease and emphysema." [17] Foote testified at the hearings and worked hard but with no visible signs of success to support the Federal Trade Commission's action.[18]

The council, on paper, looks like a powerful lobbying organization. *Barron's*, a national financial weekly, accused it of being a front for the bureaucracy, particularly the Public Health Service.[19] There is some substance to this charge. Two of the three officers of

---

League of Nursing, National Medical Association, National Student Nurses Association, National Tuberculosis and Respiratory Disease Association, Public Health Cancer Association of America, Student American Medical Association, U.S. Department of Defense, U.S. Office of Child Development, U.S. Office of Education, U.S. Public Health Service, and U.S. Veterans Administration.

[16] From a speech by Franklin B. Dryden, assistant to the president, The Tobacco Institute, Inc., before the 21st Tobacco Workers Conference, January 17–20, 1967, Williamsburg, Virginia, p. 12 (mimeo.).

[17] Roy Parker, Jr., "Ad Whiz Has New Target," *Raleigh News and Observer*, January 12, 1965.

[18] Mr. Foote was succeeded as president of the National Interagency Council by former Surgeon General Luther L. Terry, who in turn was succeeded by his former assistant surgeon general, Dr. James L. Hundley. Dr. Hundley served as assistant chairman of Dr. Terry's Advisory Committee on Smoking and Health. The council devotes most of its effort to holding conferences and promoting educational campaigns designed to discourage smokers from continuing their habit.

[19] "Best Foote Forward?," *Barron's*, January 18, 1965.

the organization during the labeling hearings were staff members of the Public Health Service and for five years the headquarters of the council was maintained at Public Health Service offices in suburban Washington. Yet, this rather impressive coalition of health organizations was no match for the cigarette manufacturers. As the date for the congressional hearings approached, it seemed that the antismoking people were politically outclassed by the cigarette group. Cigarettes had high-priced talent, exceptional political experience, a tight organization, and powerful, entrenched support in Congress. Antismoking forces lacked large measures of these vital political ingredients.

THE CONGRESSIONAL HEARINGS

The Senate Commerce Committee hearings attracted more attention than those of its counterpart committee in the House. The publicity that accompanied these hearings coupled with the fact that some of the membership of the Senate committee were uncommitted on the smoking and health issue underscored their importance. Those who supported the Federal Trade Commission rule were given favorable positions in the scheduling of their testimony, a sign that committee leadership was sympathetic to the commission's ruling. Out of courtesy, members of Congress who requested permission to testify were allowed to go first. The next time, the first slot of the second morning was given to a representative of the American Cancer Society. This early position helped to assure him of newspaper and television coverage. A spot later in the day would have drawn less public attention.

One of the difficulties that plagued the health groups throughout the congressional hearings was the absence of agreement on just what they wanted Congress to do. They agreed that cigarette smoking was harmful to health and that the government should do something about it. All of the health witnesses stressed these points. Members of Congress, bureaucrats, physicians, and the representatives of the public interest groups knew the medical arguments well and presented them with feeling. But this is where their agreement ended. Their failure to agree on a plan of action reflected their lack of political know-how and inability to organize a cohesive campaign. Senator Clements, on the other hand, had made certain the cigarette manufacturers avoided any disunity.

The disunity of the health groups became obvious early in the hearings. The Surgeon General suggested that the Federal Trade Commission was not the most appropriate agency to enforce the labeling and advertising requirement. He noted that the Department of Health, Education and Welfare could provide the type of regulatory approach required for enforcement of the cigarette labeling regulations. Chairman Dixon did not take immediate exception to the Surgeon General's point of view. Nevertheless, he did stress in his testimony the necessity of Federal Trade Commission involvement because the absence of a health warning was an unfair or deceptive trade practice. Prevention of such practices was within the jurisdiction of the Federal Trade Commission, Dixon reminded the committee.

The health forces were further split on the wording of the warnings that they wanted to appear on packages and in advertising. Senator Neuberger favored "Caution—Habitual Smoking Is Injurious to Health"; Senator Bennett and Congressman Moss would have preferred this statement: "Warning: Continual Cigarette Smoking May Be Hazardous to Your Health." A third suggested phrase was proposed by the American Heart Association: "Caution: Habitual Cigarette Smoking Frequently Constitutes a Serious Hazard to Health."

These disputes were in sharp contrast to the ultrasmooth coordination and scenario employed by the cigarette interests. The case that the cigarette people made in support of their position was a good one. Their arguments were detailed, coherent, and generally persuasive.

THE CIGARETTE MEN TESTIFY

The cigarette lobbyists' presentations before Congress were much different from the presentations they made at the Federal Trade Commission hearing. Before the congressional committees they covered all aspects of the argument: the Surgeon General's report, other studies on the health consequences of smoking, the importance of unfettered competition to the economy and the American creed, tobacco's contribution to the nation, and the proper policy role of Congress *vis-à-vis* the states and administrative agencies. This full complement of arguments contrasted sharply with the limited legal argument presented at the Federal Trade Commission hearings.

Another significant difference in approach by the tobacco forces between the Federal Trade Commission and congressional hearings was the number of witnesses who appeared for cigarettes. At the Federal Trade Commission, one lawyer represented the manufacturers. In Congress, dozens of witnesses from a variety of professional fields appeared. The testimony of these witnesses was skillfully orchestrated by Earle Clements.

The heart of the industry case was given to each of the congressional committees by Bowman Gray, chairman of the board of the R. J. Reynolds Company, a competent and effective witness. His voice never rose above conversational tones. For two hours at the witness table of each committee, he chain-smoked his way through what proved to be a thoughtful synopsis of the industry arguments that were to follow. And although Mr. Gray disclaimed any medical expertise, he carefully laid the groundwork for the prosmoking medical arguments. He touched base with the economists by noting that "unwise legislation in this field could produce repercussions which would be felt throughout the country's economy." He went on to warn that the balance of payments problem might even be exacerbated if exports of tobacco products fell.

Ideological and philosophical objections also appeared in Mr. Gray's testimony. Policy in a democracy should be made by Congress, not an administrative agency; and the will of the people embodied in their elected representatives should be supreme, he continued. On other philosophical questions, Gray argued that there was a right to advertise—a right that he labeled "an essential commercial" one. He acknowledged that he believed the Federal Trade Commission rule was "step one in the [government's] trying to get control of one industry." And he added, it was "a first step to get control of other industries."

After Mr. Gray came the parade of witnesses, the largest number of whom were medical doctors and professionals from allied fields. All of them cast doubt on the Surgeon General's report. The report, they claimed, was based on statistical rather than clinical evidence and was not sufficient proof that smoking caused diseases. A Virginia pathologist argued that the evidence "submitted . . . by proponents of the theory that lung cancer is caused by smoking . . . does not constitute scientific proof of this theory." Darrell Huff, author of *How to Lie With Statistics,* talked darkly about the Surgeon General's committee's work. He pointed to a number of statistical and methodological "warning signals" that perhaps indicated that some conclusions in the report were not warranted by the facts.

The majority of witnesses at the congressional hearings testified against the Surgeon General's report and the Federal Trade Commission's rule. Most of the professionals who testified identified their employers as independent research associations. However, nearly two years after the hearings, it was disclosed that a few of the witnesses had not properly or fully identified themselves. Senator Daniel Brewster (D.–Maryland) mailed questionnaires to those who testified on behalf of the cigarette industry. Sixteen of the 37 questionnaires he sent were returned. Some of those answering admitted that they had received large fees from the tobacco interests for their testimony. This came as a surprise to some members of the committee who thought they were hearing professional opinions untarnished by any possible financial connection with the industry. Senator Brewster suggested that there be a committee investigation of any possible conflict of interest that might have arisen at the labeling hearings. The request died quietly and quickly. Congress itself pays only the expenses of those witnesses it asks to testify; others pay their own expenses. The problem of witnesses paid by special interests is not serious so long as they disclose their connections. The problem of undisclosed connections is an ethical one; its implications remain unexplored by Congress.

Cigarette manufacturers had a number of well-organized allies in Washington. While the Senate Commerce Committee was holding its hearings, the National Association of Broadcasters held its annual convention in town. There were over 500 radio and television executives in attendance. At a reception, more than 400 of the 535 members of Congress were entertained by these executives and treated to their views on the right to advertise. It has been estimated that more than one-third of the members of Congress own major stock holdings in radio and television stations. This could account for some of the sympathy in Congress for those who were threatened by government regulation of cigarette advertising.[20]

After the hearings, the Senate Commerce Committee quickly voted down Senator Neuberger's bill to accept the Federal Trade Commission's approach to regulation of cigarette labeling and advertising. The members of the committee, instead, reported out a bill very similar in form and content to the one eventually passed into law. Senator Neuberger attempted to amend the bill on the floor, but she was unsuccessful.

The bill went to President Johnson on July 13, and he maintained his silence on the legislation as he had done throughout the controversy. On July 27, within hours of the time the bill would have become law automatically without the president's signature, it was signed. Eight disenchanted members of Congress, in league

[20] Roy Parker, Jr., "Cigarettes Have Friends in Labeling Battle," *Raleigh News and Observer,* March 25, 1965.

with lobbyists for the Americans for Democratic Action, attempted to persuade the president to veto the bill. Their efforts were to no avail. The president signed the legislation in the privacy of his office. There were no guests, no glitter, and no souvenir pens, which ordinarily accompany the signing of a major piece of legislation. The bill was signed without ceremony, and the president's press secretary released the news without benefit of comment.

The passage of the Cigarette Labeling and Advertising Act marked the end of a well-organized campaign to move Congress to adopt an unusual oversight measure. The skills of the Tobacco Institute, enhanced by the sympathies of many members, helped to remove any doubts that might have existed in the Federal Trade Commission or elsewhere as to where ultimate policymaking authority resided. Congress is effective in disciplining errant agency policymakers, particularly when those agencies challenge the interests of powerful economic groups. Although the lengths to which Congress went to discipline the Federal Trade Commission were unusual, it is not unusual for members to prevent similar agency actions through less stringent, more informal methods.

THE FEDERAL TRADE COMMISSION RESCINDS ITS RULE

The day after the president signed the bill, the Federal Trade Commission issued an order vacating its trade regulation rule. In this order, the commissioners took note of the fact that the legislation did not change the findings or conclusions that were the basis of the labeling and advertising rule. Manufacturers were warned that any advertising that attempted to undermine the warning that was required on packages would be unfair and deceptive and could be stopped by the commission. Although the legislation prohibited the Federal Trade Commission from requiring a health warning, the July 28 commission order stated, "[The commission] will continue to monitor current practices and methods of cigarette advertising and promotion, and take all appropriate action consistent with the Act to prohibit cigarette advertising that violates the Federal Trade Commission Act." [21]

The legislation marked the end of a turbulent excursion into congressional politics for the Federal Trade Commission. In the summer of 1965, the commission settled down to its more normal routine and put to one side, at least temporarily, any plans for mounting a new rulemaking proceeding in the cigarette and health field until the ban against its doing so expired in the summer of 1969. The commission set up its tar and nicotine laboratory and began gathering information for its yearly reports to Congress on cigarette smoking and advertising. Although things around the Federal Trade Commission grew quieter, the cigarette controversy continued. The nonsmoking genie was out of the bottle, and it began to appear and reappear in other, often unexpected, places. Congress had succeeded in silencing the Federal Trade Commission for a while, but it was about to hear from some of her sister agencies on the same subject in slightly different garb. The congressional action had won cigarette manufacturers some time, but the question of smoking, its relationship to health, and what the government might do about it was far from settled.

[21] "Vacation of Warning Requirements in Trade Regulation Rule Concerning Advertising and Labeling of Cigarettes," 30 *Federal Register,* p. 9484 (1965).

8

CONGRESS
AND THE BUREAUCRACY:
A BALANCE OF POWER?

The struggle between Congress and the Federal Trade Commission was resolved only temporarily in favor of Congress by the moratorium imposed in the Cigarette Labeling and Advertising Act. The commission, joined by its newly acquired health constituency and other bureaucratic agencies, succeeded in keeping the cigarette controversy alive despite the congressional action designed to temporarily curtail the FTC's power. The agencies continued to work for acceptance of the idea of requiring a health warning in advertising even though the congressional ban against making such a requirement remained in effect until July 1, 1969.

In the years since Congress chose to exercise its oversight prerogative, the agencies have enlisted public support, found an ally in the Federal Communications Commission, and achieved more unity in pressuring for their goal of strengthening the health warning and extending it to advertising. On the other hand, the political strength of the tobacco companies has eroded slightly as new health studies trace even more serious medical consequences to cigarette smoking. The position of the manufacturers has deteriorated further in the eyes of many because the manufacturers have not voluntarily altered the direction of their advertising campaigns, which still portray smoking as good clean fun. The FTC claims that cigarette manufacturers are continuing to promote their products as harmless prerequisites to social acceptability.

The introduction of the 100-millimeter cigarettes in 1967–68— giving the smoker more smoke, generally with higher tar and nicotine content, for the same price as regular or king-size cigarettes— was taken by some members of the commission as proof of the callous disregard by the manufacturers for government attempts to curtail smoking.

BUREAUCRACY CONTINUES THE CONTROVERSY

The Public Health Service continued its efforts to reduce smoking through its National Clearinghouse for Smoking and Health and by the appointment of two advisory panels. The first group, composed of 14 experts, was asked by the Surgeon General to review recent medical research dealing with the effects of tar and nicotine on health. The panel reported that the scientific evidence suggested that lower tar and nicotine content in cigarette smoke reduced the harmful effects of smoking. This disclosure came shortly after Senator Magnuson had asked the Federal Trade Commission to reverse its ban on including tar and nicotine disclosures in advertising. He had also asked the commission to establish a laboratory to measure the quantities of these ingredients in every brand.[1] The

[1] William G. Meserve, staff counsel to the Senate Commerce Committee, discussed some of these developments in a speech titled, "Cigarettes and Congress," before the California Conference on Cigarette Smoking and Health, October 29, 1967.

commission quickly agreed to the senator's request and installed, in its headquarters' building, machines that smoke cigarettes and measure the amount of tar and nicotine in each one. The results of these tests are published regularly and distributed by the commission. Manufacturers have been encouraged to include the test results in their advertising, and since early 1971 all of them have done so.

In the fall of 1967, the Surgeon General created a second panel —the Task Force on Smoking and Health—which included ex-advertising man and health interest convert Emerson Foote and retired baseball star Jackie Robinson. The task force captured considerable public attention when, in August 1968, it reported that some gains had been made in that the increasing rate of consumption had been slowed somewhat. Nonetheless, the task force condemned the industry for the content of its advertisements and asked the government for more stringent regulations, including the requirement of a health warning in advertising. The report was sufficiently critical of cigarette manufacturers to elicit this response from the Tobacco Institute: "[This report is] . . . a shockingly intemperate defamation of an industry which has led the way in medical research to seek answers in the cigarette controversy." [2]

The 1965 Cigarette Labeling and Advertising Act provided some opportunity for the bureaucracy to keep attention focused on the smoking and health issue through the requirement that both the Federal Trade Commission and the Public Health Service submit annual reports to Congress on smoking. According to the act, these reports were to contain current information concerning smoking and health together with recommendations for further legislative action. The reports provided an opportunity for both agencies to make very strong appeals for further action to curb smoking. Both the 1967 and 1968 reports of the Department of Health, Education and Welfare called for warnings to appear in advertising along with the disclosure of tar and nicotine content. Secretary of Health, Ed-

[2] Victor Cohn, "Smoking Crisis: U.S. Task Force Asks Funds for Fight on Cigarette Ads," *The Washington Post*, August 17, 1968.

ucation and Welfare Wilbur J. Cohen appointed in the spring of 1968, concluded his letter to Congress with these words: "In my opinion, the remedial action taken until now has not been adequate." The letter was accompanied by a lengthy bibliography and analysis of the hundreds of medical articles and research studies published since the Surgeon General's 1964 report. The HEW acted much more aggressively in the cigarette health field under Secretary Cohen than it did in 1965 at the height of the controversy.

The HEW reports have grown increasingly strong on the adverse effects of smoking. The 1972 report hit a peak when it concluded for the first time that nonsmokers exposed to the cigarette smoke of others were being exposed to a health hazard. The report indicates that it is no longer enough to give up smoking; one has to stay out of rooms or other closed places where other people are smoking.

The Federal Trade Commission also seems to have been encouraged rather than intimidated by the rebuke it suffered at the hands of Congress. In addition to its speedy action in setting up the tar and nicotine laboratory, the commission has submitted hard-hitting reports to Congress. The first report, submitted in June 1967, contained five recommendations. These included a requirement that a warning statement appear in all advertising and that the statement itself be made stronger. The report suggested changing the warning to read: "Warning: Cigarette Smoking Is Dangerous to Health and May Cause Death from Cancer and Other Diseases." Furthermore, the commission called for more appropriations for itself and for the HEW to increase its campaigns to bring the antismoking message to the public with greater effectiveness.

The commission's second report was even bolder than its first. It contained some analysis of advertising content and an exposé of what the Federal Trade Commission felt was a blatant attempt to mislead the public. An article by Stanley Frank appeared in the January 15, 1968 issue of *True Magazine* dismissing the evidence against smoking as inconclusive and inaccurate. Less than two months later an article with similar conclusions appeared in the *National Enquirer* titled, "Cigarette Cancer Link Is Bunk." It was written by Charles Golden. Within a few days the *Wall Street Journal* disclosed that the articles were placed in these two national publications by the tobacco interests. Stanley Frank and Charles Golden were the same person—who later became a staff member of the public relations firm retained by the Tobacco Institute. The institute ordered more than one million reprints of the *True* article, which were mailed to doctors, medical researchers, educators, and nearly every member of Congress. The FTC estimated that this campaign cost the institute at least $175,000. This journalistic-public relations episode led the commission to conclude that these actions were ". . . not the acts of an industry either confident of its facts nor solicitous of its reputation." [3]

Perhaps it was this obvious attempt by the tobacco manufacturers to discredit the government's work in the smoking field that stiffened the Federal Trade Commission's position in its 1968 *Report to Congress*. The 1968 report contained a recommendation that was not included the previous year. The commission recommended that cigarette advertising on television and radio be banned entirely. If the advertising could not be banned, the commission suggested that the hours at which such advertisements appear be limited and that the total amount of advertising also be regulated. The report was adopted by the FTC with only one dissenting vote. Commissioner Nicholson and Chairman Dixon noted in concurring opinions that they hoped the government would not have to go so far as to impose a ban on radio and television advertising. Yet even they were adamant in their expressions of need for more stringent requirements, particularly the requirement that a health warning appear in all advertising. In later years the FTC reports continued to argue for radio and television ad bans as well as the requirement that a strengthened health warning be included in printed advertising.

Probably the most important event to occur during the four-year moratorium on the Federal Trade Commission was the dra-

---

[3] Federal Trade Commission, *Report to Congress,* June 30, 1968, p. 30 (mimeo.).

matic entrance of the Federal Communications Commission (FCC) into the smoking and health controversy. This commission, like the other independent regulatory bodies, has generally shown very little interest in moving against the wishes of those it regulates. Yet, with relatively little prodding, the FCC was persuaded to require that broadcasters air antismoking publicity more frequently. The FCC's action favoring the antismoking people, against the wishes of the broadcasting industry, is interesting politically because of the very limited support it had in any quarter, including the health groups themselves.

The requirement for more antismoking publicity was adopted when the Federal Communications Commission was persuaded to apply its fairness doctrine to cigarette commercials. Application of the fairness doctrine in this case meant that any station that carried cigarette ads was obliged to give the public the other side of the issue, that is, inform them of the health hazards in smoking. The FCC was prompted to act when it received a letter from a young New York lawyer, John F. Banzhaf, III. Mr. Banzhaf requested that the commission require WCBS-TV in New York City to give free, to responsible health groups, the same amount of time as that sold to tobacco companies for the purpose of promoting the virtues and values of smoking. The FCC did not require that precise amounts or exactly equal time be given, but it did require stations to provide "a significant amount of time for the other viewpoint." [4]

The commission's decision came as a surprise to nearly everyone. The president of the National Association of Broadcasters called the action an "unwarranted and dangerous intrusion into American business. . . ." [5] Members of Congress were caught off guard by the FCC's announcement. One tobacco-state congressman, Walter Jones (D.–North Carolina), attempted to rally support for the cigarette manufacturers among other industries, the advertising of whose products he claimed might in the future meet a fate at the

[4] Federal Communications Commission, Public Notice, 1188-B, June 5, 1967 (mimeo.).

[5] "Wasilewski Opposes Fairness Doctrine Being Applied to Cigarette Spots," *TV Code News*, Volume 6, No. 6, June, 1967, p. 3.

hands of the FCC similar to that of cigarette advertising. He warned that other groups, for example, those opposing the consumption of alcoholic beverages, might soon request that the fairness doctrine be applied to them. Senator Magnuson, on the other hand, announced his support for the FCC action, terming it a major victory for health forces.

There was some surprising opposition, or at least nonsupport, for the FCC action from some of the health groups. While the initial reaction of these groups was favorable, they later started having misgivings, which surfaced when appeals were filed in the U.S. Court of Appeals for the District of Columbia by two Washington law firms—Covington and Burling and Arnold and Porter—on behalf of the cigarette manufacturers.[6] The misgivings of groups like the American Cancer Society were based on the fear that the courts might agree with the complaint and dismiss the FCC opinion. They would then be in the position of having been antagonistic to radio and television stations and the networks. The Cancer Society and its allies knew that they were dependent upon the owners of the stations and the networks for the free announcements that promoted their own fund-raising drives. They chose a prudent course in this legal struggle, hoping to avoid putting their good will and free time with station owners in jeopardy. Consequently, health group support for the FCC was quiet and nonaggressive, and even nonexistent. The fears of the health groups were unjustified, for on November 21, 1968, the U.S. Court of Appeals decided that the FCC could use its fairness doctrine to require free time for antismoking commercials.[7]

An amusing variety of antismoking ads began to appear on radio and television. Informative and dramatic, it seems certain that they contributed to the reduction in cigarette consumption noted

6 John F. Banzhaf, III, is executive director of an organization called ASH (Action on Smoking and Health), that endeavored to raise a legal defense fund of $100,000 to help protect and defend the FCC's decision. Among the sponsors of ASH are many of those individuals associated with the antismoking forces, including Maurine Neuberger.

7 *John F. Banzhaf, III v. Federal Communications Commission,* 405 F. 2d. 1082 (1968).

first in 1968. The Federal Communications Commission's ruling helped the health groups get their message aired. The American Cancer Society reported that in the three and one-half years before the FCC applied its fairness doctrine to cigarette ads, it distributed a total of 982 prerecorded antismoking commercials for radio and television. In the eight months after the FCC's decision, the Cancer Society distributed 4,723 such commercials.[8]

The work of Banzhaf in persuading the FCC to apply the fairness doctrine to cigarette commercials was one of the most significant events in the whole labeling controversy. The total ban on airwave advertising that became effective in 1971 won the support of the cigarette manufacturers largely because they wanted to avoid the "anti" commercials. As the ad ban began, the FCC ruled that television and radio stations could carry antismoking commercials as a "public service" after the ban became operative but would not be required to carry the opposite views of the cigarette companies. This seemed unfair to the manufacturers, who decided to appeal the FCC's rule to the courts, where they were rebuffed.[9]

Banzhaf, Nader, and the numerous organizations they have created and inspired are frequent users of the policymaking powers of administrative agencies to bring about changes in policy favorable to consumers. Crusades to eliminate dangerous products from the marketplace and deceptive practices in advertising rely on agency action for their support. The consumer movement that began in the 1960s has given greater force to administrative law as a tool of social change. The procedures and the laws that agencies use for policymaking are not new for the most part. What is new is their use by organized, professionally staffed consumer groups. Agency power marshalled for the consumer is often less than enthusiastically

8 Robert E. Dallos, "Perry Mason's TV Foe, Dead of Cancer, Left Anti-Smoking Film," the *New York Times,* September 13, 1968, p. 55.

9 By April 1972, with cigarette commercials no longer broadcast, very few antismoking announcements were being aired. In an interview reported in the *Richmond Times-Dispatch* April 23, 1972, Dr. Daniel Horn, director of the National Clearinghouse on Smoking and Health, said, "Thank goodness they're off the air. The antismoking advertisements had outlived their usefulness. They were beginning to have a backlash effect."

received by Congress, as in the cigarette controversy. A recent study notes, ". . . the administrative process has proved to be the key element in consumer protection policy and the implementation of that policy invariably has taken a different path than that envisioned by the original proponents of the legislation." [10] The agencies and Congress define their agendas differently in the field of consumer protection.

As the July 1, 1969 expiration date of the Cigarette Labeling Act of 1965 approached, the cigarette controversy began appearing on the agendas of government agencies again. The Federal Communications Commission unexpectedly announced in February 1969 a proposed rule that would prohibit cigarette advertising on radio and television. The commission said it would not act before July 1, thereby indicating to Congress that if it allowed the 1965 act to expire, cigarette advertising would be restricted to periodicals and newspapers.

The FCC announcement at a news conference and in the *Federal Register* put Congress on notice that it would have to take some action before the July 1 expiration date. There were several paths this action could have taken. Congress could have chosen not to act at all, allowing the 1965 legislation to expire. This would have permitted the FCC to adopt the rule it had proposed in February and would also have allowed the Federal Trade Commission to act if it so desired. On the other hand, Congress could have extended the ban on agency action incorporated in the 1965 legislation, or it could have passed almost any bill strengthening or weakening the health warning label, including a requirement that it appear in all advertising.

The antismoking interests found themselves in an unusually good position, because for once they could advance their cause by seeing that Congress failed to act. If Congress could be persuaded to remain silent, the health interests thought their desires would be implemented by agencies released from the congressional ban

[10] Mark V. Nadel, *The Politics of Consumer Protection* (Indianapolis: Bobbs-Merrill, 1971), p. 29.

on rulemaking. Senator Frank E. Moss, Democrat of Utah and a longtime advocate of strenuous action against the health hazards of cigarette smoking, put the Senate on notice as to what his strategy would be, in a speech on January 31, 1969:

> For the first time, the legislative advantage lies with the public. It is the cigarette industry which has the burden of getting Congress to act. If there is no new legislation extending the ban on agency regulation, then the agencies will again be free to act on July 1.
>
> . . . I want to serve notice here and now that I shall do all within my power to see that no such law to continue the ban passes.
>
> Although, as my colleagues know, I have long and steadfastly opposed rules which make it possible for a small group of Senators to prevent the passage of legislation through a filibuster, when it comes to a matter involving the lives and health of millions of Americans, I shall not hesitate to take full advantage of the existing rules, and to enlist the support of my many colleagues of like mind in the Senate— and there are many—to stop the passage of "disabling" legislation.[11]

Congressional inaction proved to be a highly unrealistic desire. The tobacco lobby was prepared for the expiration date. The House Interstate and Foreign Commerce Committee held 13 days of hearings in April and May, two months before the ban was due to expire. The 1969 hearings were a repeat of their 1965 predecessors. The tobacco industry position was again carefully and skillfully orchestrated before the committee. Most of the arguments and many of the witnesses were the same as those used in 1965. Michael Pertschuk, chief counsel for the Senate Commerce Committee and intimately involved in the cigarette controversy from the earliest days when he was on Senator Maurine Neuberger's staff, sensed history repeating itself:

> There is a new President and a new party in the White House and there is a new Congress. But, there is nothing in this new Congress to suggest a weakening of the proportionate strength of tobacco-state

11 *Congressional Record*, January 31, 1969, p. S1124.

congressmen. Ten congressmen out of the thirty-six on the House
Interstate and Foreign Commerce Committee came either from tobacco-growing districts or districts closely allied politically and economically with those tobacco-growing districts.[12]

The bill reported out of the committee and passed by the
House on June 18 was a nightmare for the health interests. It prohibited the states permanently, and federal agencies for six more
years, until July 1, 1975, from acting on cigarette advertising, in exchange for a slightly strengthened warning, which would replace
the existing warning on packages.

The reaction in the Senate and elsewhere in government was
severe. The tobacco interests were regarded as having overplayed
their hand. What followed was a good example of politics extended
beyond the usual subsystem. Numerous agencies, public and private,
state and national, began to propose policies favorable to the health
interests. In June, the California Senate voted to ban all cigarette
advertising in California, the *New York Times* announced it would
no longer carry cigarette ads without health warnings and the FTC
started its hearings on a revival of its trade regulation rule on July 1,
the day the original congressional ban expired.

By the time the Senate hearing was held on July 22, 1969, the
tobacco interests sensed that their victory in the House was too unpopular to stand. They retreated strategically in the face of certain
Senate opposition led by their powerful critics Senators Moss and
Magnuson.

The Senate Commerce Committee's Consumer Subcommittee,
chaired by Senator Moss, held the hearing. In the Senate there were
few parallels with 1965. This time it was a short, one-day hearing.
Only five tobacco witnesses appeared. Joseph Cullman III, chairman
of the Tobacco Institute's executive committee, announced that
the cigarette manufacturers were willing to withdraw all radio and
television advertising beginning January 1, 1970, provided Congress

[12] Michael Pertschuk, "A Look Backward and A Glance Forward," *A Summary of Proceedings,* National Interagency Council on Smoking and Health,
September, 1970, p. 22.

would extend antitrust immunity to cover an intercompany agreement to do so. From that point on, the tobacco interests adopted a statesmanlike posture. Voluntary action and lack of opposition to congressional action characterized their public positions. The bill that emerged from Congress the following March banned cigarette ads from radio and television beginning January 2, 1971 in lieu of an antitrust provision, and strengthened the warning on packages. One concession to the tobacco interests was the provision that the Federal Trade Commission had to give Congress six months' notice of any rulemaking activity affecting cigarettes. Another provision of the act gave the FTC the authority to consider the warning requirement for all printed advertising after July 1, 1971. Preemption of state action was continued.

Six radio station owners appealed the broadcast prohibition to the courts. In March 1972, the Supreme Court upheld the congressional action. The cigarette manufacturers did not join in the appeal.

Two important voluntary agreements were reached between the FTC and the cigarette manufacturers after the passage of the act. The companies agreed to list tar and nicotine content in all advertising, and they also agreed to reproduce in all printed advertising the health warning that would be printed on cigarette packs. The FTC was not completely satisfied with the latter agreement, so on July 1, 1971, the first day the legislation of 1970 permitted the commission to do so, the FTC announced that it would proceed against the cigarette companies individually for false and deceptive advertising unless they included a more "clear and conspicuous" reproduction of the health warning in printed advertising. This procedure allowed the FTC to avoid the congressional sensitivity against cigarette rulemaking. A consent order was signed in January, 1972, in which the manufacturers agreed to place the warning in their printed advertising.

Eight years after the Surgeon General issued his report and the FTC announced its rulemaking, the policy that the FTC had proposed was adopted. The cigarette manufacturers were discovering that agreement with the antismoking people was not such a bad thing. The advertising budgets of the manufacturers dropped an estimated 30 percent in 1971, the first year of the TV and radio ad ban, and gross sales were up 3 percent.[13]

The cigarette labeling controversy continues, but on a substantially lower key. Senator Moss hopes to persuade the Food and Drug Administration that it has the power to limit the tar and nicotine content of cigarettes produced in this country under the Hazarduous Substances Act. If the FDA is unwilling to set limits, he plans to attempt to do so through a court suit or the passage of new legislation. A related issue concerned the appearance of little cigars that look a lot like cigarettes. Cigars were not covered by the government's restrictions on cigarettes. The manufacturers called upon the government for a more precise definition of "cigarette" to differentiate cigarettes from other tobacco products, which had escaped the regulatory fate of cigarettes. On September 10, 1973, legislation was signed that included little cigars in the cigarette advertising ban.

The tobacco subsystem was changed completely in eight years. The small group of people in Congress, in the agencies, and in the tobacco groups lost control of the policymaking processes. As they did, very remarkable changes in public policy occurred. The cigarette labeling issue will fade from public view, and as it does, a new subsystem will emerge. The new tobacco subsystem is likely to be a much different one from that which preceded it and was powerful until the early 1960s.

THE BUREAUCRACY AND CONGRESS IN POLICYMAKING

The initiation and continuation of the cigarette controversy were possible because of both the political power and delegated authority possessed by bureaucratic agencies. Had the decision on cigarettes and health been left to Congress alone, it is safe to assume that

[13] *Tobacco Situation,* Washington, D.C.: Economic Research Service, U.S. Department of Agriculture, March 1972.

the manufacturers would have triumphed and no health warning of any kind would have been required. The cigarette labeling controversy is a clear example of agencies' powers to influence and even formulate public policy.

The Tobacco Institute was aware that the challenge to its interests was from the bureaucracy and not from Congress. It recognized the political benefits to be gained in arguing that there was in this situation an apparent divergence between the way policy actually was being made and the manner in which traditional theories of representation suggested policy should be made. The cigarette manufacturers emphasized the point that the FTC did not have, or at least should not have, the power to make policy. They argued that policymaking was the prerogative of Congress alone. On the surface, this position seems valid and has attracted support from many quarters over the years. Groups or individuals who think their interests are threatened by agency action frequently adopt the narrow view that agencies, under the Constitution, are prohibited from policymaking. Some argue that bureaucrats are merely the servants of Congress, and the lack of full congressional control of bureaucracy is a serious obstacle to democratic control.[14]

The master-servant view of the relationship between Congress and the bureaucracy is no longer tenable from either a practical or a legal perspective. In practice, the demands of a complex society require the specialized skills of bureaucrats in policymaking. The principle of congressional delegation of policymaking authority has been accepted by the courts.

Criticisms of bureaucratic policymaking powers are made on the grounds that bureaucrats might act capriciously, unchecked by public opinion or other governmental institutions, and undisciplined by the rigors of standing for election. Whether or not the decisions of agencies are unchallenged depends on the political environment in which the agency is situated. If the environment provides challenges to bureaucratic decisions, there should be little fear

---

[14] See Charles S. Hyneman, *Bureaucracy in a Democracy* (New York: Harper and Brothers, 1950) for a comprehensive exposition of this point of view.

of capricious agency action. However, an abundance of safeguards does not guarantee responsive government, because their ready availability frequently makes it easier for small, special interest groups to stop proposed changes in policy. A wide range of safeguards restrained the Federal Trade Commission during the cigarette labeling controversy. There were pressures from Congress including both hearings and legislation. The commission used formal hearing procedures in adopting its rule, thereby encouraging public participation in decision making. There was also the threat, and real possibility, of judicial review. Furthermore, a series of informal, more subtle devices were at work restraining any tendency that might have existed within the Federal Trade Commission toward capricious action.[15]

At the national level there are numerous ways to check agency power. Capricious or arbitrary action is not as serious a problem in national government as it is in local governments and in some foreign governments where political institutions are often too weak or disorganized to challenge the bureaucracy. The problem in Washington is more often one of persuading the bureaucracy to act when it knows from experience that doing as little as possible reaps the greatest benefits. Hardening of administrative arteries is more serious than agency aggressiveness.

Not only does the bureaucracy operate in an environment of highly developed political constraints, but it is also, in many ways, a representative institution. Practical experience has cast some doubts on the theory that democratic representation can only be achieved through elections. One might argue that Congress has in theory the best chance of being the most representative institution of government because it is dependent on the electoral process. Yet, studies of voters, elections, and the power structure of Congress have demonstrated that Congress frequently falls short of representative ideals. One-party jurisdictions, the seniority system, and concentra-

---

[15] Charles E. Gilbert discusses the wide variety of controls over agency policy-making in "The Framework of Administrative Responsibility," *Journal of Politics,* Volume 21, August, 1959, pp. 373–408.

tion of power in congressional committees make it difficult, if not impossible, for a majority to work its will inside or outside Congress.

The bureaucracy is probably no more representative than Congress, but it does have some representational qualities. Measured in terms of social and economic factors, the federal bureaucrats are more representative of the nation as a whole than members of Congress. One well-known political scientist has compared bureaucrats to congressmen in this way:

> . . . the bureaucracy now has a very real claim to be considered much more representative of the American people in its composition than the Congress. This is not merely the case with respect to the class structure of the country, but, equally significantly, with respect to the learned groups, skills, economic interests, races, nationalities, and religions. The diversity that makes up the United States is better represented in its civil service than anywhere else.[16]

Both the operation and organization of the federal bureaucracy help to reinforce its representativeness. Decision making is diffused among many individuals and agencies. There is considerable overlapping of functions making it difficult for any single agency to capture and hold for itself an area of policy over long periods of time. Challenges to agency predominance in almost any field are frequent. In the cigarette controversy, there was very little agreement on policy between the Department of Agriculture, which has the tobacco farmers as constituents, and the FTC. There was even disagreement *within* the Department of Health, Education and Welfare when the Public Health Service took a position quite different from the secretary of the department. Another challenge to agency predominance can be exercised by the president or, as is more frequently the case, by the Office of Management and Budget, which is directly under his control.

The existence of a bureaucracy with policymaking powers assures a more broadly representative decision-making process than

[16] Norton E. Long, "Bureaucracy and Constitutionalism," *The American Political Science Review,* Volume 46 (September, 1952), pp. 808–819.

one that relies solely on a legislature. Bureaucrats, if they wish, can afford to take a somewhat broader view of an issue because they are not directly answerable to a narrow constituency as are most congressmen. Congressmen generally have to respond to specialized interests, particularly when those interests are well organized in their constituency.[17] How an institution of government operates alone is not so important as how it works in concert with other institutions. The combination of bureaucratic and congressional policymaking powers can make important contributions to a system in which expanded participation in democratic policymaking is the goal.

Often agencies fail to make positive contributions to representation because they respond only to the small, powerful interest groups upon which they depend for their political strength. The private citizen's ability to influence government can be thwarted by an agency's myopic allegiance to the industry or persons over whom it exercises jurisdiction just the same as it might be thwarted in the halls of Congress. Although bureaucratic policymaking powers might increase the competition among special interest groups, they do very little to enhance the individual's ability to influence his government. The existence of these powers does make it possible on occasion for some groups, even poorly organized ones, to break the grip of powerful interests on government. On the other hand, the time, money, and energy required to gain government acceptance of the cigarette health warning illustrate that those who are poorly organized and poorly financed make advances very slowly, even with the assistance of agency policymaking powers.

[17] This position is well argued by Peter Woll in *American Bureaucracy* (New York: W. W. Norton and Company, 1963).

Chronology
of Important Events
in the Cigarette Labeling
Controversy

1939	The first scientific study of smoking and lung cancer published.
1950 through 1954	Fourteen major studies completed, all of which link cigarette smoking and serious diseases. The first prospective study, begun in 1951, receives much publicity both while in progress and when the results are published on August 7, 1954.
January 3, 1954	Cigarette manufacturers set up Council for Tobacco Research—U.S.A. (originally called Tobacco Industry Research Committee).

March 6, 1957

Four health organizations issue a report citing causal relationship between cigarette smoking and lung cancer and call for government action.

July 18, 19, 23, 24, 25, 26, 1957

First congressional hearings on smoking and health held by the Legal and Monetary Affairs Subcommittee of the House Government Operations Committee, John A. Blatnik (D.–Minnesota), chairman.

January, 1958

Tobacco Institute, Incorporated, established by major United States cigarette manufacturers.

October 28, 1962

Surgeon General announces appointments to the Advisory Committee on Smoking and Health.

November 9, 1962

Advisory Committee holds its first session.

January 11, 1964

Advisory Committee releases its report to the public.

January 18, 1964

Federal Trade Commission issues its official notice of rulemaking pertaining to the advertising and labeling of cigarettes (29 *Federal Register* 530–532, January 22, 1964).

January 27, 1964

The Public Health Service announces its acceptance in full of the Advisory Committee's report. Distribution of free cigarettes to the 16 Public Health Service Hospitals and 50 Indian Hospitals is discontinued. (The Veterans' Administration and the Department of Defense soon followed suit in their medical installations.)

February, 1964	Several congressmen introduce legislation related to the controversy and call for hearings.
February, 1964	National Association of Broadcasters amends its television advertising code to discourage portrayal of cigarette smoking as a habit worthy of imitation by youngsters.
March 16, 17, 18, 1964	Hearings held before the Federal Trade Commission.
April 27, 1964	Cigarette manufacturers announce the establishment of their voluntary Cigarette Advertising Code.
May 15, 1964	Deadline for filing written data with the Federal Trade Commission to be included in the cigarette labeling and advertising hearing record.
June 22, 1964	Federal Trade Commission promulgates its Trade Regulation Rule on Cigarette Labeling and Advertising. (29 FR 8325, July 2, 1964.)
June 23, 24, 25, 29 and July 2, 1964	Hearings held before the House Committee on Interstate and Foreign Commerce.
July, 1964	Coalition of health groups, the National Interagency Council on Smoking and Health, established.
August 19, 1964	Chairman Oren Harris (D.–Arkansas) of House committee asks Chairman Paul Rand Dixon of the Federal Trade Commission to delay implementation date of ruling. Chairman Dixon agrees. (Effective date had been scheduled, January 1, 1965.)

March 22, 23, 24, 25, 29, 30, and April 1, 2, 1965	Hearings held before the Senate Committee on Commerce.
April 6, 7, 8, 9, 13, 14, 15, and May 4, 1965	House hearings completed.
June 16, 1965	Cigarette labeling bill passes in Senate.
June 22, 1965	Bill passes in House.
June 28, 1965	Tobacco Institute announces it will defer court action challenging FTC rule because of what it considered favorable congressional support for its position.
July 6, 1965	Senate agrees to report of the House-Senate Conference Committee.
July 13, 1965	House agrees to conference report.
July 27, 1965	President signs the bill.
October, 1965	Congress appropriates funds to establish the National Clearinghouse for Smoking and Health in the Public Health Service.
January 1, 1966	Health warning labels appear on all cigarette packages.
June 5, 1967	Federal Communications Commission rules that fairness doctrine applies to cigarette advertising.
June 30, 1967	Federal Trade Commission in its first report to Congress after passage of labeling act claims warning should be required in cigarette advertising.

August, 1967	Senator Robert F. Kennedy introduces legislation to require a health warning in all cigarette advertising and to give the Federal Trade Commission power to regulate times and types of programs on which cigarette ads might appear and control over total volume of cigarette ads. The bill also proposes greater taxes on cigarettes with higher tar and nicotine content.
November 22, 1967	Federal Trade Commission releases tar and nicotine content of 59 brands as determined in their new testing laboratory.
June 30, 1968	Federal Trade Commission restates its views to Congress on health warnings in advertising.
July 1, 1968	Secretary of Health, Education and Welfare Wilbur J. Cohen asks Congress to extend health warnings to advertising.
November 21, 1968	U.S. Court of Appeals upholds the Federal Communication Commission's application of fairness doctrine to cigarette advertising.
February 5, 1969	Federal Communications Commission proposes rule to ban all cigarette advertising from radio and television.
April 15, 16, 17, 18, 21, 22, 23, 24, 25, 28, 29, 30, and May 1, 1969	House Interstate and Foreign Commerce Committee holds hearings of cigarette legislation. Ninety members of Congress had introduced or cosponsored bills.
May 20, 1969	Federal Trade Commission issues notice of rulemaking hearings (to begin July 1) to require more forceful health warning on

cigarette packages and to extend the warning requirement to all advertising.

June 5, 1969

House Interstate and Foreign Commerce Committee reports out bill to extend ban on agency and state government action in cigarette field to 1975. Adopts more forceful language for package labels.

June 18, 1969

The committee's bill passes in the House.

June 25, 1969

California Senate votes to ban cigarette advertising in newspapers and magazines published in California as well as on state radio and TV stations.

June 30, 1969

Congressional ban on agency and state government action in the smoking and health field expires.

July 1 and 2, 1969

FTC holds hearings on a new health warning and extension of the warning to advertising.

July 7, 1969

Television Code Review Board of the National Association of Broadcasters endorses phasing out of cigarette ads on radio and television by September 1, 1973.

July 22, 1969

Consumer Subcommittee of the Senate Commerce Committee holds hearings on cigarette labeling and advertising legislation.

August 22, 1969

The *New York Times* states in an editorial that all cigarette ads in its pages after January 1970 must carry the health warning currently required on all cigarette packages.

September 5, 1969	R. J. Reynolds, Philip Morris, and the American Tobacco Company announce they will no longer advertise in the *New York Times*.
December 5, 1969	Senate Commerce Committee reports bill to bar cigarette advertising from the airwaves starting January 1, 1971. The bill also prohibits FTC action on cigarette advertising until July 1, 1971. (The House passes a six-year moratorium.)
December 12, 1969	The committee bill passes in the Senate.
March 3, 1970	House and Senate conferees agree to ban ads from radio and television beginning January 2, 1971. Also agree to allow the FTC to consider requiring warnings in printed advertising after July 1, 1971 if the commission deems it necessary. Package label changed to: "Warning: The Surgeon General Has Determined that Cigarette Smoking Is Dangerous to Your Health." Under the act, the FTC must give Congress six months' notice of any pending rulemaking concerning cigarettes.
March 19, 1970	Congress passes the new labeling act called the Public Health Cigarette Smoking Act of 1969.
April 1, 1970	The legislation is signed by President Nixon.
May 19, 1970	World Health Organization takes a public position against cigarette smoking. This action marks widespread international support for the antismoking movements, which have been growing rapidly in most Western countries.

July 31, 1970

The Cigarette Advertising Code, a voluntary organization supported by cigarette manufacturers and directed by Robert B. Meyner (former governor of New Jersey), goes out of business. Manufacturers see no need for the organization any longer.

December 1, 1970

Six radio station owners file suit to enjoin the government from enforcing the new legislation, which would ban cigarette advertising from the airwaves beginning the following month, January 1971.

December 15, 1970

Federal Communications Commission rules that television and radio stations may continue to carry antismoking commercials, but they will not be required to carry prosmoking ads under the provisions of the fairness doctrine. Manufacturers appeal the decision to the courts. At the same time, the FCC refuses to require broadcasters to carry antismoking commercials after the ad ban begins in January.

December 17, 1970

Cigarette manufacturers volunteer to include disclosure of tar and nicotine content of cigarettes in all advertising. Agreement to take effect 60 days later.

December 22, 1970

FTC sets aside a regulation that would have required tar and nicotine disclosures in the light of the industry's voluntary action to include this information in advertising.

January 1, 1971

Last day for cigarette advertising on radio and television.

January 11, 1971

Surgeon General proposes government initiative to ban smoking in public places. Nonsmokers in smoke-filled rooms experience a health hazard, he claims.

January 27, 1971

Bill introduced to terminate direct and indirect price subsidies to tobacco farmers.

February 3, 1971

FTC again asks Congress to legislate stiffer package warning label and to require health warning in printed advertising.

February 6, 1971

Voluntary agreement on listing of tar and nicotine content in all advertising becomes operative.

February 22, 1971

Bill introduced in Congress to ban smoking in all but certain designated areas in airliners, trains, and buses.

March 10, 1971

Bill introduced in Congress to prohibit sending unsolicited cigarette samples through the mail.

March 14, 1971

Chairman Kirkpatrick of the FTC discloses a letter to Senator Moss noting that the commission is considering a requirement that a health warning be included in all printed advertising.

April 1, 1971

Bill introduced that would set limits for tar and nicotine content of cigarettes.

April 15, 1971

Seven of nine major cigarette companies agree voluntarily to include health warning in all printed advertising. To begin immediately.

June 24, 1971

FTC announces its intent to proceed against cigarette companies for false and deceptive advertising to force inclusion of health warnings in all printed advertising. The commission notes its dissatisfaction with the voluntary agreement reached with the companies on April 15, 1971.

July 1, 1971

Congressional prohibition against FTC rulemaking in cigarette regulation expires. The commission announces it will sue six of the major cigarette manufacturers if they do not begin including a "clear and conspicuous" health warning in all advertising.

October 20, 1971

U.S. Court of Appeals holds that the congressional ban on radio and television advertising does not violate the First or Fifth Amendment rights of station owners. The owners file an appeal to the Supreme Court.

January 31, 1972

Six major cigarette companies agree, under a consent order with the FTC, to include a "clear and conspicuous" health warning in all cigarette advertisements. To become operative in six months.

February 1, 3 and 10, 1972

Senate Commerce Subcommittee on Consumer Affairs holds hearings on various aspects of cigarette regulation.

February 7, 1972

Secretary of HEW issues policy directive to establish no smoking rules in departmental conference rooms, auditoriums, sections of cafeterias, and in certain work areas.

February 10, 1972

The National Clearinghouse for Smoking and Health moves within HEW to become a part of the department's Center for Disease Control. The reorganization indicates emphasis of the point of view that smoking is a preventable health problem.

March 27, 1972	Supreme Court upholds congressional action banning cigarette commercials from radio and television.
April 4, 1972	U.S. District Court declares that FTC lacks statutory authority to issue trade regulation rules in case involving posting of octane ratings on gasoline pumps.
January 29, 1973	FTC refuses to ban "little cigars" from radio and television, urging Congress to amend the 1970 Cigarette Labeling and Advertising Act.
February 15, 16, 1973	Under congressional pressure, Lorillard and Reynolds Tobacco companies withdraw their little cigar ads from radio and TV; Consolidated Cigar Corporation refuses.
March 19, 22, 27, 28, 29, 30, 1973	House Subcommittee on Commerce and Finance begins hearings on a bill (HR 20) which would reaffirm the FTC's rulemaking authority.
April 3, 1973	Senate Commerce Committee reports out a bill to ban little cigar ads from radio and TV.
April 30, 1973	Senate passes ban on little cigars.
June 19, 1973	House Interstate and Commerce Committee holds hearings on little cigars.
June 27, 1973	The U.S. Court of Appeals upholds the rulemaking authority of FTC in case involving

the posting of octane ratings on gasoline pumps.

June 28, 1973

Senate Banking and Currency Committee reports out a bill (S 356) that would improve FTC's consumer protection activities, deleting at the request of the FTC a section reaffirming FTC's rulemaking authority.

September 10, 1973

The ban on little cigar ads becomes Public Law 93-109.

January 14, 1974

Total prohibition of cigarette advertising on billboards requested in a petition filed before the Federal Trade Commission.

February 25, 1974

Supreme Court denies certiorari in the octane case thereby allowing to stand the U.S. Court of Appeals decision confirming the FTC's rulemaking authority.

Federal Trade Commission's Trade Regulation Rule on Cigarette Labeling and Advertising (29 FR 8325)

SUBCHAPTER D—TRADE REGULATION RULES

PART 408

Unfair or deceptive advertising and labeling of cigarettes in relation to the health hazards of smoking

Part 408 is added to Chapter I, Title 16, Code of Federal Regulations, reading as set forth below.

The Federal Trade Commission, pursuant to the Federal Trade Commission Act, as amended, 15 U.S.C. sections 41, et seq., and the provisions of Subpart F of the Commission's Procedures and Rules of Practice, 28 F.R. 7083-84 (July 1963), has conducted a proceeding for the promulgation of a Trade Regulation Rule, or Rules, for the prevention of unfair or deceptive acts or practices in the sale of cigarettes. Notice of this proceeding, including a set of proposed Rules, was published in the FEDERAL REGISTER on January 22, 1964 (29 F.R. 530-532). Interested parties were thereafter afforded an opportunity to participate in the proceeding through the submission of written data, views and argument and to appear and express orally their views as to the proposed rules and to suggest revisions thereof and amendments and additions thereto. In adopting this rule, the Commission has given due consideration to all such views, data and argument together with all other relevant matters of fact, law, policy and discretion.

Sec. 408.1   The rule.
   408.2   Definitions.
   408.3   Petition to reopen rulemaking proceeding.
   408.4   Effective dates.

AUTHORITY: The provisions of this Part 408 issued under Federal Trade Commission Act, as amended; 38 Stat. 717, as amended; 15 U.S.C. 41-58; 16 CFR 1.61-1.67.

§ 408.1   The rule.

The Commission, on the basis of the findings made by it in this proceeding, as set forth in the accompanying Statement of Basis and Purpose of Trade Regulation Rule, hereby promulgates as a trade regulation rule its determination that in connection with the sale, offering for sale, or distribution in commerce (as "commerce" is defined in the Federal Trade Commission Act) of cigarettes it is an unfair or deceptive act or practice within the meaning of section 5 of the Federal Trade Commission Act (15 U.S.C. § 45) to fail to disclose, clearly and prominently, in all advertising and on every pack, box, carton or other container in which cigarettes are sold to the consuming public that cigarette smoking is dangerous to health and may cause death from cancer and other diseases.

§ 408.2   Definitions.

For purposes of the rule in this part:
(a) "Cigarette" means any roll of tobacco wrapped in paper or otherwise commonly considered a cigarette.

(b) "Advertising" includes all radio and television commercials, newspaper and magazine advertisements, billboards, posters, signs, decals, matchbook advertising, point-of-sale display material, and all other written or other material used for promoting the sale or consumption of cigarettes, but does not include the labeling of packs, boxes, cartons and other containers in which cigarettes are sold to the consuming public.

§ 408.3   Petition to reopen rulemaking proceeding.

In the event that any person subject to the rule in this part is of the opinion that new or changed conditions of fact or law, the public interest, or special circumstances require that the rule in this part be suspended, modified, waived, or repealed as to him, or otherwise altered or amended, such person may file with the Secretary of the Commission a petition to reopen this rulemaking proceeding, stating the changes desired and the grounds therefor. The Commission will act on the petition as provided in § 1.66 of this chapter (the Commission's Procedures and Rules of Practice).

§ 408.4   Effective dates.

(a) Except with respect to advertising, the rule in this part shall become effective on January 1, 1965.

(b) With respect to advertising, the rule in this part shall become effective on July 1, 1965: *Provided, however,* That the Commission will entertain an application filed prior to May 1, 1965, by any interested party to postpone the effective date or otherwise suspend, modify, or abrogate the provisions of the rule in this part as to advertising, upon a showing of such change in circumstances as to justify such requested action in the public interest.

Issued: June 22, 1964.
By the Commission.   JOSEPH W. SHEA,
[SEAL]   *Secretary*

SUGGESTIONS FOR FURTHER READING

ANDERSON, JAMES E., *Politics and the Economy.* Boston: Little, Brown and Company, 1966.

APPLEBY, PAUL, *Big Democracy.* New York: Alfred A. Knopf, 1945.

BAILEY, STEPHEN K., *Congress Makes a Law: The Story Behind the Employment Act of 1946.* New York: Columbia University Press, 1950.

BAUER, RAYMOND A., ITHIEL DE SOLA POOL, and LEWIS ANTHONY DEXTER, *American Business and Public Policy: The Politics of Foreign Trade.* New York: Atherton Press, 1963.

BENDINER, ROBERT, *Obstacle Course on Capitol Hill.* New York: McGraw-Hill Book Company, 1964.

BERMAN, DANIEL M., *A Bill Becomes a Law: Congress Enacts Civil Rights*

Legislation, Second Edition. New York: The Macmillan Company, 1966.

BERNSTEIN, MARVER H., *Regulating Business by Independent Commission.* Princeton, N.J.: Princeton University Press, 1955.

BLAU, PETER M., *Bureaucracy in Modern Society.* New York: Random House, 1956.

BOYER, WILLIAM W., *Bureaucracy On Trial: Policy Making by Government Agencies.* Indianapolis: The Bobbs-Merrill Co., 1964.

CARY, WILLIAM L., *Politics and the Regulatory Agencies.* New York: Mc-Graw-Hill Book Company, 1967.

COX, EDWARD F., ROBERT C. FELLMETH, and JOHN E. SCHULZ, *The Nader Report on the Federal Trade Commission.* New York: Grove Press, Inc., 1969.

CRAIN, ROBERT L., ELIHU KATZ, and DONALD B. ROSENTHAL, *The Politics of Community Conflict.* Indianapolis: The Bobbs-Merrill Co., 1969.

CUSHMAN, ROBERT E., *The Independent Regulatory Commission.* New York: Oxford University Press, 1941.

DAVIS, JAMES W., JR., *Little Groups of Neighbors: The Selective Service System.* Chicago: Markham Publishing Company, 1968.

DAVIS, KENNETH CULP, *Administrative Law and Government.* St. Paul, Minnesota: West Publishing Company, 1960.

————, *Discretionary Justice: A Preliminary Inquiry.* Urbana, Illinois: University of Illinois Press, 1969.

DROR, YEHEZKEL, *Public Policymaking Reexamined.* San Francisco: Chandler Publishing Co., 1968.

FREEMAN, J. LEIPER, *The Political Process: Executive Bureau-Legislative Committee Relations.* New York: Random House, 1965.

FROMAN, LEWIS A., JR., *People and Politics: An Analysis of the American Political System.* Englewood Cliffs, N.J.: Prentice-Hall, Inc., 1962.

GRIFFITH, ERNEST S., *Congress: Its Contemporary Role,* Third Edition. New York: New York University Press, 1961.

HARRIS, JOSEPH P., *Congressional Control of Administration.* New York: Doubleday Anchor Books, 1965.

HARRIS, RICHARD, *The Real Voice.* New York: The Macmillan Company, 1964.

HENDERSON, GERARD C., *The Federal Trade Commission: A Study in Ad-*

ministrative Law and Procedure. New Haven, Conn.: Yale University Press, 1924.

HERRING, PENDLETON, *Public Administration and the Public Interest.* New York: McGraw-Hill Book Company, 1936.

HYNEMAN, CHARLES S., *Bureaucracy in a Democracy.* New York: Harper and Brothers, 1950.

JACOB, CHARLES E., *Policy and Bureaucracy.* New York: D. Van Nostrand Co., 1966.

JONES, CHARLES O., *An Introduction to the Study of Public Policy.* Belmont, Calif.: Wadsworth Publishing Co., Inc., 1970.

KOHLMEIER, LOUIS M., JR., *The Regulators: Watchdog Agencies and the Public Interest.* New York: Harper and Row Publishers, 1969.

KRISLOV, SAMUEL, and LLOYD D. MUSOLF, *The Politics of Regulation: A Reader.* Boston: Houghton Mifflin Co., 1964.

LANE, ROBERT E., and DAVID O. SEARS, *Public Opinion.* Englewood Cliffs, N.J.: Prentice-Hall, Inc., 1964.

LEISERSON, AVERY, *Administrative Regulation: A Study in Representation of Interests.* Chicago: University of Chicago Press, 1942.

LONG, NORTON E., *The Polity.* Chicago: Rand McNally Co., 1966.

LOWI, THEODORE J., *The End of Liberalism: Ideology, Policy, and the Crisis of Public Authority.* New York: W. W. Norton Co., Inc., 1969.

MAGNUSON, WARREN G., and JEAN CARPER, *The Dark Side of the Market Place.* Englewood Cliffs, N.J.: Prentice-Hall, Inc., 1968.

MASON, LOWELL, *The Language of Dissent.* Cleveland: The World Publishing Company, 1959.

MCCONNELL, GRANT, *Private Power and American Democracy.* New York: Alfred A. Knopf, Inc., 1966.

MINTZ, MORTON, and JERRY S. COHEN, *America, Inc.: Who Owns and Operates the United States.* New York: The Dial Press, 1971.

MITCHELL, WILLIAM C., *The American Polity: A Social and Cultural Interpretation.* New York: The Free Press, 1962.

MOSHER, FREDERICK C., *Democracy and the Public Service.* New York: Oxford University Press, 1968.

MUND, VERNON A., *Government and Business,* Fourth Edition. New York: Harper & Row Publishers, 1965.

NADEL, MARK V., *The Politics of Consumer Protection*. Indianapolis: The Bobbs-Merrill Co., Inc., 1971.

NEUBERGER, MAURINE B., *Smoke Screen: Tobacco and the Public Welfare*. Englewood Cliffs, N.J.: Prentice-Hall, Inc., 1963.

PENNOCK, J. ROLAND, *Administration and the Rule of Law*. New York: Rinehart and Company, Inc., 1941.

POWELL, NORMAN JOHN, *Responsible Public Bureaucracy in the United States*. Boston: Allyn and Bacon, Inc., 1967.

PRICE, DON K., *Government and Science: Their Dynamic Relationship*. New York: New York University Press, 1954.

———, *The Scientific Estate*. Cambridge, Mass.: Harvard University Press, 1965.

RANNEY, AUSTIN (ed.), *Political Science and Public Policy*. Chicago: Markham Publishing Co., 1968.

REDFORD, EMMETTE S., *American Government and the Economy*. New York: The Macmillan Company, 1965.

———, *Democracy in the Administrative State*. New York: Oxford University Press, 1969.

ROURKE, FRANCIS E., *Bureaucracy, Politics, and Public Policy*. Boston: Little, Brown and Company, 1969.

ROURKE, FRANCIS E., ed., *Bureaucratic Power in National Politics*. Boston: Little, Brown and Company, 1965.

SCHATTSCHNEIDER, E. E., *The Semi-Sovereign People*. New York: Holt, Rinehart and Winston, 1960.

SCHOOLER, DEAN, JR., *Science, Scientists, and Public Policy*. New York: The Free Press, 1971.

SCHWARTZ, BERNARD, *The Professor and the Commissions*. New York: Alfred A. Knopf, 1959.

SHARKANSKY, IRA, (ed.), *Policy Analysis in Political Science*. Chicago: Markham Publishing Co., 1970.

WILDAVSKY, AARON, *The Politics of the Budgetary Process*. Boston: Little, Brown and Company, 1964.

WOLL, PETER, *American Bureaucracy*. New York: W. W. Norton and Co., 1963.

INDEX

Abell, Bess, 24
Action on Smoking and Health (ASH), 39, 146n
Adjudication (administrative)
  compared with rulemaking, 70–72, 74, 75
  FTC, 72–77
Administrative Conference of the United States, 57n
Administrative law judges
  in adjudication, 103, 104
  civil service status, 104, 105
  duties, 101, 102
  history, 102, 103
  number of, 100, 101
  in rulemaking, 105
Administrative Procedure Act (APA), 82–84, 103–4, 112, 113

Advertising Federation of America, 10
Advisory Committee on Smoking and Health, viii, 42–49, 78, 81, 121
  membership, 44n
  political nature, 42, 43
  procedures, 46
  report, 9, 19n, 47, 48
  selection of, 43–45
Advisory committees
  control, 50–52
  types, 42
Advisory opinions, FTC, 73
Agriculture, Department of, 4, 31, 32, 155
Allen, George V., 23
American Bar Association, 79
American Cancer Society, 19, 43n, 130, 131n, 133, 146, 147

American Heart Association, 19n, 130, 134
American Medical Association, 22n, 130n, 131n, 143n
American Newspaper Publishers Association, 10
American Political Science Association, 115
American Tobacco Company, 29, 61
American Tobacco Company v. United States, 61n
Americans for Democratic Action, 129, 138
Arnold and Porter, 24, 146
Association of National Advertisers, 10, 95
Austern, H. Thomas, 93–96

Banzhaf, John F., III, 39, 145, 146n, 147
Bass, Ross, 128
Bennett, Wallace, 123n, 134
Blatnik, John A., 27
Bolling, Richard, 123, 124n
Boyer, William W., 13n, 45n
Brewster, Daniel, 136
Brown and Williamson Tobacco Corporation (FTC proceedings), 32n
Bureaucracy, vii
  conflict within, 30–36
  part of subsystem, 4, 5, 9–16
  policymaking, 11–13, 40, 41, 140, 153–56
  size, 30
Business Advisory Council, 49, 50

Carper, Jean, 20n, 38n
Cary, William L., 66, 67n
Cater, Douglass, 5n
Celebrezze, Anthony, 33–35
Cigarette Advertising Code, 23, 107, 108, 120
Cigarette Labeling and Advertising Act of 1965, 120–25, 138, 140, 142, 148
Cigarettes
  advertising, 8, 10, 25, 31–33, 74–77, 89, 107–10, 151
  ban on advertising, 137–39, 144, 145, 148, 150, 151
  congressional hearings, 27, 127, 128, 135–37
  consumption, 2, 9, 20, 33
  deaths attributed to, 19, 20

Cigarettes (*continued*)
  early legislation, 26
  expenditures for, 6, 25
  FTC hearings, 74–77, 81, 88–99
  government promotion of, 31, 32
  health related research, 17–21, 143
  introduction of, 7, 8
  regulation of advertising, 74–77, 137, 138
  sales, 2, 8, 9, 48
  suits against manufacturers, 28–30
Civil Service Commission, 103–5
Clare, Donald, 12n
Clark, Joseph, 123n
Clayton Act, 63
Clements, Earle C., 23, 24, 125, 126, 135
Code of Federal Regulations, 106
Cohen, David, 129
Cohen, Wilbur J., 143
Cohn, Victor, 142n
Commerce, Department of, 49, 50
Committee on Commerce (Senate), 124, 126–28, 133, 150
Congress
  cigarette bills, 26
  committees, 4, 5, 27n, 126, 127, [*See also* Committee on Commerce (Senate); Interstate and Foreign Commerce Committee (House)]
  delegation of authority, 11, 53–59, 94, 95
  health power in, 129–34
  members before FTC, 92
  oversight functions, 115–20
  part of subsystem, 4–6
  tobacco power in, 26, 109, 127
Consent order, 73, 74
Consumer
  legislation, v, 38, 80n
  protection, 11, 68, 147, 148
Cordtz, Dan, 34n
Coser, Lewis, 6n
Council for Tobacco Research—U.S.A., 22
Covington and Burling, 93, 146
Cox, Edward F., 79n
Cronin, Thomas E., 45n
Cullman, Joseph, 150

Dallos, Robert E., 147n
Davis, Kenneth Culp, 58n
Dawson, William L., 27n
Delegation of authority
  congressional, 11, 53–59, 94, 95

Delegation of authority (*continued*)
  reasons for, 53–57
  standards for, 65, 66
  Supreme Court decisions, 58, 61, 64–66
Democratic Study Group, 123, 124
Dicey, A. V., 111
Dirksen, Everett, 115
Division of Trade Regulation Rules, FTC, 81
Dixon, Paul Rand, 78, 90, 109, 130, 134, 144
Donovan, Robert J., 49n
Douglas, Paul, 123n
Drew, Elizabeth Brenner, 125n, 129n
Dryden, Franklin B., 8n, 132n
Dullea, Charles, 65n

Elman, Philip, 22, 76, 90, 95
Evans, Rowland, 24n

Fahey v. Mallonee, 65n
Fairness doctrine, 145–47
Federal Advisory Committee Act of 1972, 50, 51
Federal Advisory Committee Report, 51
Federal Communications Commission (FCC), 140, 145–48
Federal Register, 85, 86, 106, 107
Federal Trade Commission (FTC)
  adjudication and rulemaking compared, 72–74
  advertising guidelines, 32, 33, 76
  advertising regulation, 75–77, 138
  ban on cigarette advertising, 89, 144
  congressional oversight, 12, 93, 109, 117–20
  hearings on cigarettes, 76n, 87, 89–96
  informal procedures, 72–74
  judicial review, 67, 68, 80
  powers limited, 67
  reports to Congress, 22, 76n, 105n, 108n, 143, 144
  rule on cigarette labeling, viii, 12, 52, 78–82, 84, 106, 138, 144n
  rulemaking, ix, 69, 72, 77–81, 98
  studies of, 79
Federal Trade Commission v. Curtis Publishing Company, 67n
Federal Trade Commission v. Klesner, 67
Federal Trade Commission v. Raladam, 67n

Federal Trade Commission v. Ruberoid, 56n, 57n
Federal Trade Commission v. Warren, Jones and Gratz, 67n
Fellmeth, Robert C., 79n
Ferber, Mark F., 124n
Field v. Clark, 64n
Food and Drug Administration (FDA), 33–35, 152
Foote, Emerson, 132
Fortas, Abe, 24
Frank, Stanley, 143
Freeman, J. Leiper, 4n
Freeman, Orville, 31
Fur Products Labeling Act, 94, 96

Gaskill, Nelson B., 67n
Gilbert, Charles E., 154n
Golden, Charles, 144
Gray, Bowman, 135, 136
Green v. American Tobacco Company, 29n
Greenberg, D. S., 10n
Griffith, Ernest S., ix, 4n
Guthrie, Eugene, 44

Hammond, E. Cuyler, 18
Harris, Joseph P., 117n
Harris, Oren, 109, 123
Harris, Richard, 35n
Hartke, Vance, 128
Hazardous Substances Labeling Act, 35, 152
Health, Education and Welfare, Department of (HEW), 33, 34, 122, 131, 134, 142, 143, 155
Health warning label, viii, 1, 9–12, 20, 30, 36, 89, 119, 121, 122, 134, 143, 148
Hearing examiners (*see* Administrative law judges)
Hearings, congressional
  Committee on Commerce, 133–37
  Government Operations Committee, 27, 50
  health testimony, 133, 134
  tobacco testimony, 135–37
Hearings, FTC
  commissioners' role, 87, 90–93, 95, 99, 100
  health testimony, 92
  tobacco testimony, 93–97
  witnesses, 91–93

Hearings, FTC (*continued*)
(*See also* Federal Trade Commission
and Cigarettes)
Henderson, Gerard C., 61n
Hill and Knowlton, 126
Hockett, Robert C., 21n
Horn, Daniel, 18, 147n
Huff, Darrell, 136
Hyneman, Charles S., 153n

Independent agencies, defined, 66
Interstate and Foreign Commerce Committee (House), 34, 52, 123, 127, 149, 150, 151
Interstate Commerce Commission (ICC), 62, 96n, 102, 103, 114

Johnson, Lyndon B., 24, 36, 121, 125, 137
Jones, Mary Gardiner, 90
Jones, Walter, 145
Judicial proceedings
suits against cigarette manufacturers, 28–30
under Sherman Act, 60–62
Judicial review of administration
Administrative Procedure Act, 104
common law, 110, 111
law v. fact, 112, 113
procedures, 113
Justice, Department of, 60

Kefauver, Estes, 35, 92
Kennedy, John F., 40, 41
Kennedy, Robert F., 12, 108, 123n, 138
Kilbourne v. Thompson, 64n
Kornegay, Horace, 127

Label (*see* Health warning label)
Leiserson, Avery, 45n
Liggett and Myers Tobacco Company (FTC proceedings), 32n
Loevinger, Lee, 56, 57
Long, Norton E., 130n, 155n
Lowi, Theodore J., 13n

McConnell, Grant, 50n
MacIntyre, Everette A., 91
McLellan, David S., 12n
Magnuson, Warren, 20n, 38n, 108, 124, 140, 141, 146, 150
Meserve, William G., 141n
Metcalf, Lee, viiin

Meyner, Robert B., 107, 108
Miller, Clem, 15n
Morton, Thruston, 128
Moss, Frank, 149, 150, 152
Moss, John, 123, 134
Musolf, Lloyd D., 102n

Nadel, Mark V., 148n
Nader, Ralph, v, 39, 79, 147
National Association of Broadcasters, 10, 137, 145
code, 107, 108
National Cancer Institute, 19n
National Clearinghouse for Smoking and Health, 122, 141
National Heart Institute, 19n
National Interagency Council on Smoking and Health, 131–33
National Petroleum Refiners Association v. Federal Trade Commission, 80
National Tuberculosis Association, 43n, 130
Nelson, Gaylord, 123n
Neuberger, Maurine, 26n, 31, 34, 40, 44n, 78, 92, 128, 129, 134
Nicholson, James M., 144
Novak, Robert, 24n

Oberdorfer, Don, 46n
Office of Management and Budget
federal advisory committees, 51
legislative clearance, 15, 36
policymaking, 15, 51, 155
Office of Science and Technology, 43n
Office of the Legislative Counsel (Congress), 14n

Panama Refining Company v. Ryan, 58n, 85n
Parker, Roy, Jr., 132n, 137n
Penn Tobacco Company (FTC proceedings), 75n
Pertschuk, Michael, 149, 150
P. Lorillard and Company v. Federal Trade Commission, 68n
Policymaking process, v, vii, 3, 36–38
administrative agencies, 5, 11–14, 36, 53–59
agencies and Congress, 14–16, 115–18
agenda making, 36, 37
Office of Management and Budget, 15, 51, 155

Post Office, Department of, 12
President (see Johnson, Lyndon B.;
    Kennedy, John F.; Office of Man-
    agement and Budget
Prohibition of cigarette sales, 8
Public Health Cancer Association, 19
Public Health Cigarette Smoking Act
    of 1969, 119
Public Health Service (PHS), 18, 20,
    33, 34, 41–43, 46, 47, 52, 78, 92,
    131–33, 141, 155
Public interest, 3, 11, 55, 65

Radio Advertising Bureau, 10
Ramspeck et al. v. Federal Trial Ex-
    aminers Conference et al., 105n
Redford, Emmette S., 118n
Reilly, John, 90
Reynolds, R. J., Company, 48n, 135
Robinson, Jackie, 142
Rockefeller, Nelson A., 121
Rulemaking
    Administrative Procedure Act, 82–84
    compared with adjudication, 71–74
    FTC, ix, 69, 77–81, 98
    FTC procedures, 77–81, 98, 99

Schattschneider, E. E., 6n
Schechter Poultry Corporation v.
    United States, 58n
Schulz, John E., 79n
Schwartz, Bernard, 118n
Sears, Roebuck and Company v. Fed-
    eral Trade Commission, 65n
Securities and Exchange Commission
    (SEC), 66, 98
Securities and Exchange Commission v.
    Chenery Corporation, 98n
Senate Democratic Campaign Fund, 24,
    128
Senate Democratic Policy Committee,
    24
Separation of powers, 3, 64, 65
Shapiro, David L., 70n
Sherman Act, 60–62
Silver v. Federal Trade Commission,
    68n
Simmel, Georg, 6n
Sinclair, Andrew, 9n
Sinclair, Upton, 39
Smoking (see Cigarettes; Tobacco)
Smoking and Health (see Advisory
    Committee on Smoking and Health)
Staggers, Harley, 127

Standard Oil Company v. United
    States, 61n
State legislation on smoking, 9, 121, 122
Stewart, William H., 20
Subsystem, ix, 4–6, 38
    tobacco, 6, 12, 120, 150, 152
Supreme Court
    administrative law judges, 104, 105
    delegation, 64, 65
    FTC, 67, 68
    public notification, 85
    rulemaking, 98
    (see also Judicial review of admin-
    istration)
Surgeon General, viii, 20, 34, 43, 51, 92,
    132n (see also Advisory Committee
    on Smoking and Health)
Sweeney, Louise, 107n, 126n

Tar and nicotine, 21, 76, 77, 141, 142
Task Force on Smoking and Health,
    142
Terry, Luther L., 34, 42, 51, 132n
Thomas, Norman, 45n
Tobacco
    expenditures for, 6
    FDA regulation, 35
    government promotion of, 31
    major producing states, 26
    subsystem, 6, 12, 120, 150, 152
    (see also Cigarettes)
Tobacco Industry Research Committee
    (see Council for Tobacco Research
    —U.S.A.)
Tobacco Institute, Inc., 8n, 23, 25, 43n,
    58, 93, 96n, 120, 126n, 142, 144, 150,
    153
Trade Practices Conference, 73, 76
Trade regulation rules, 58, 59, 77, 91n
    (See also Rulemaking; Federal
    Trade Commission)

Unfair trade practices, 67
United States v. Chicago, Minneapolis
    and St. Paul Railroad Company,
    65n

Warning (See Health warning label)
Wegman, Richard A., 28n
Wheeler-Lea Act, 68
Weil, Gilbert, 95
Woll, Peter, 13n, 156n

Young, Oran R., 4n